WORKBOOK

HARCOURT SCIENCE

Harcourt School Publishers

Orlando • Boston • Dallas • Chicago • San Diego

www.harcourtschool.com

Printed in the United States of America

ISBN 0-15-313178-0

26 27 28 29 30 31 32 1421 15 14 13 12 11 10

Contents

UNIT A Plants and Animals All Around

Chapter 1—Living and Nonliving Things WB1–WB5

Chapter 2—All About Plants WB6–WB12

Chapter 3—All About Animals WB13–WB25

UNIT B Living Together

Chapter 1—Plants and Animals Need One Another WB26–WB32

Chapter 2—A Place to Live WB33–WB41

UNIT C About Our Earth

Chapter 1—Earth's Land WB42–WB48

Chapter 2—Earth's Air and Water WB49–WB55

UNIT D

Weather and the Seasons

Chapter 1—Measuring Weather WB56–WB64

Chapter 2—The Seasons WB65–WB73

UNIT E

Matter and Energy

Chapter 1—Investigate Matter WB74–WB86

Chapter 2—Heat and Light WB87–WB95

UNIT F

Energy and Forces

Chapter 1—Pushes and Pulls WB96–WB106

Chapter 2—Magnets WB107–WB115

Vocabulary Cards WB117–WB156

Name ______________________________

Reading Science

Use this checklist with every chapter of *Harcourt Science* and other science books.

When I read my science book

	Always	Sometimes
1. I use the table of contents.	☐	☐
2. I use the index at the back of the book.	☐	☐
3. I read the titles of chapters and lessons.	☐	☐
4. I look for the headings.	☐	☐
5. I look at pictures, and I read captions.	☐	☐
6. I look for and read charts and diagrams.	☐	☐

Name ____

Reading Harcourt Science

Use this checklist with every chapter of *Harcourt Science.*

When I read my science book

	Always	Sometimes
1. I read the sentences that have words with yellow boxes around them. These sentences tell the meaning of the words.	☐	☐
2. I use the picture glossary to find the meaning of words.	☐	☐
3. I read the science skill tips. They tell me about skills like *observe* and *compare.*	☐	☐
4. I read the labels on photos and diagrams.	☐	☐
5. I read to find the answers to the questions at the end of each lesson.	☐	☐
6. I list questions about what I want to know. As I read, I look for the answers.	☐	☐

Name ______________________________

What Are the Parts of a Plant?

1. Label each plant part. Use the words in the box.

roots	stem	leaves	flower

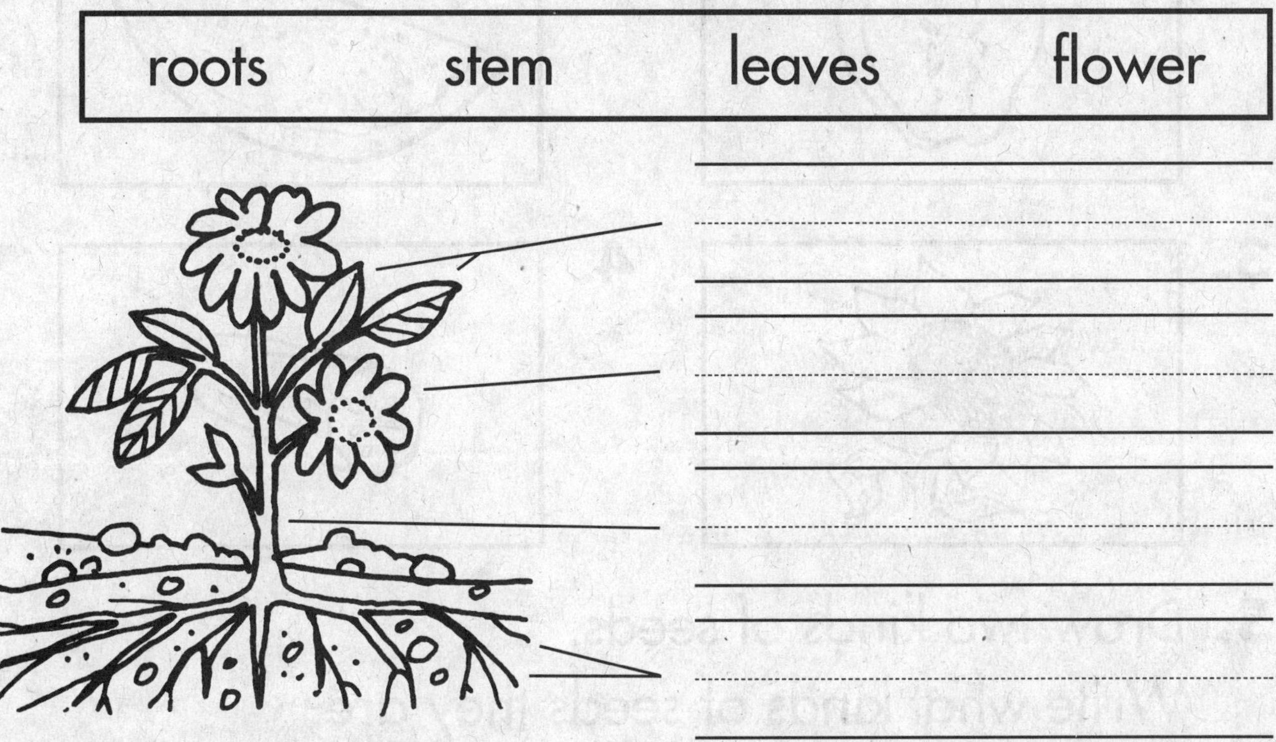

2. Color the plant part that makes food **green**.

3. Color the plant part that holds the plant in soil and takes in water **yellow**.

4. Color the plant part that moves water from the roots to the leaves **brown**.

5. Color the plant part that makes seeds **red**.

Name ______________________

Observe

Circle the seeds in each picture.

1. 

2. 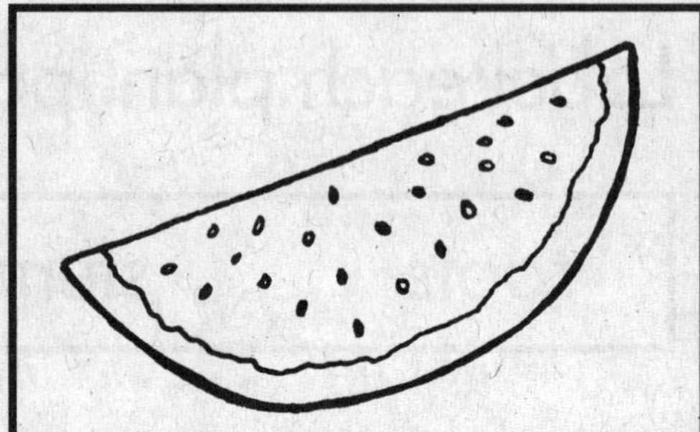

3. 

4. 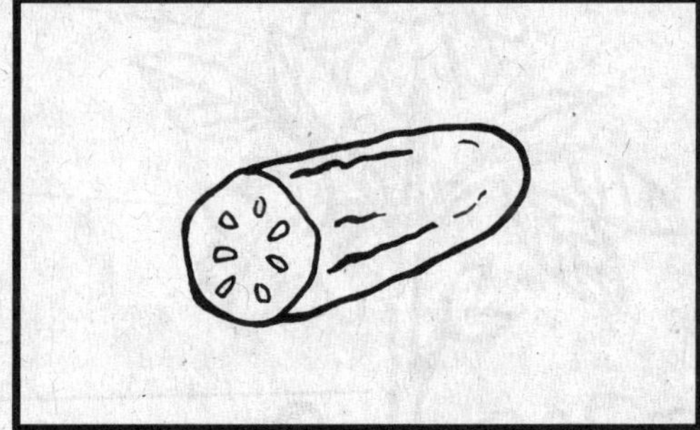

5. Draw two kinds of seeds.
Write what kinds of seeds they are.

______________________ ______________________

Use with page A28.

Name ___________________________

How Do Plants Grow?

1. This is a flower seed. What might the plant look like when it grows?

2. This is a pumpkin seed. What might the plant look like when it grows?

3. Color all the things that grew from seeds.

Name ______________________________

Communicate

1. Draw and color a plant. Show a partner the different parts of your plant.

Tell two things that all plants need. Add these things to your drawings.

2. ______________________ **3.** ______________________

 Use with page A32.

Name ______________________

What Do Plants Need?

1. Plants need air to grow. Circle two other things that plants need to grow.

2. The plant near the window is growing well. The plant in the corner is **not** growing well. Tell why.

____

____

Name ______________________

All About Plants

Write your answers. Use the words in the box.

flower	leaves	roots
stem	seed	seed coat

1. I hold plants in the soil. What am I?

2. I help hold up the plant. What am I?

3. I make food. What am I?

4. I make seeds. What am I?

5. Most plants grow from this.

Harcourt

Use with pages A38–A39.

Name ____________________

Observe

Each animal is meeting a need. Tell which need. Use words from the box.

shelter	air	water	food

1. ____________________

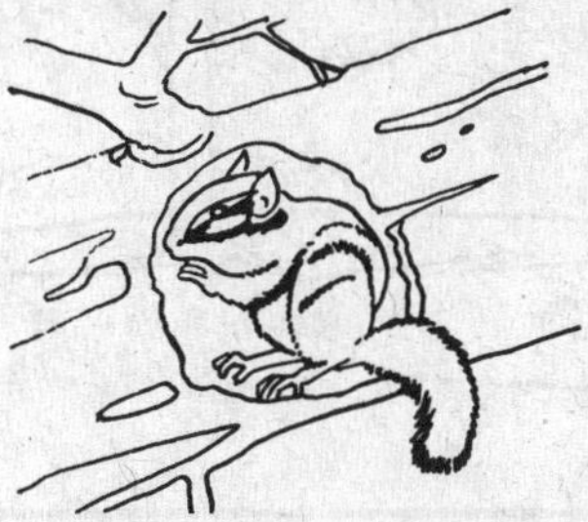

2. ____________________

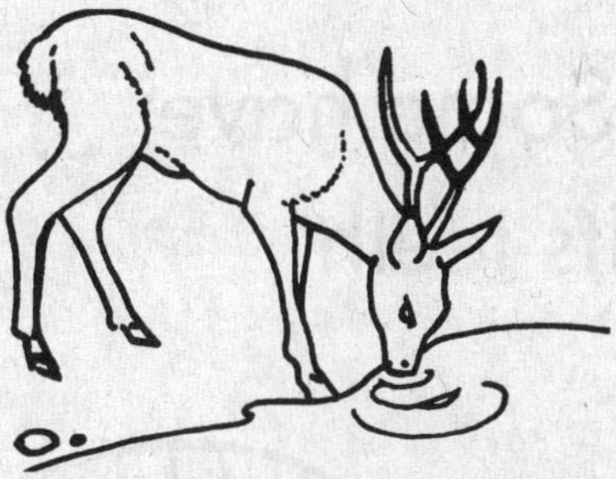

3. ____________________

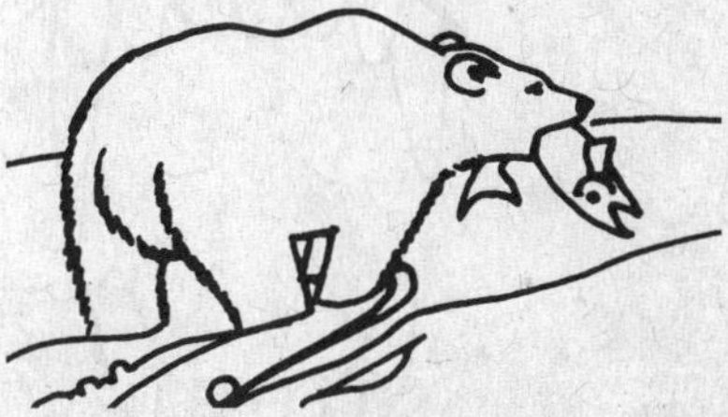

4. Draw an animal. Show it meeting its needs.

Harcourt

Name ______________________

What Do Animals Need?

1. Animals need air. Color three other things this bird needs to live.

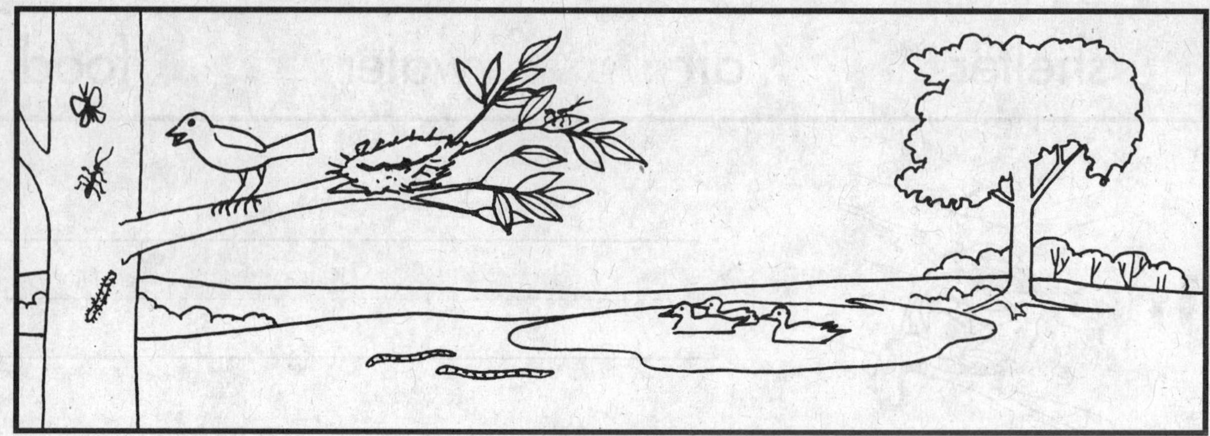

Some animals have sharp teeth. Some have flat teeth. Match each animal to its teeth.

2.

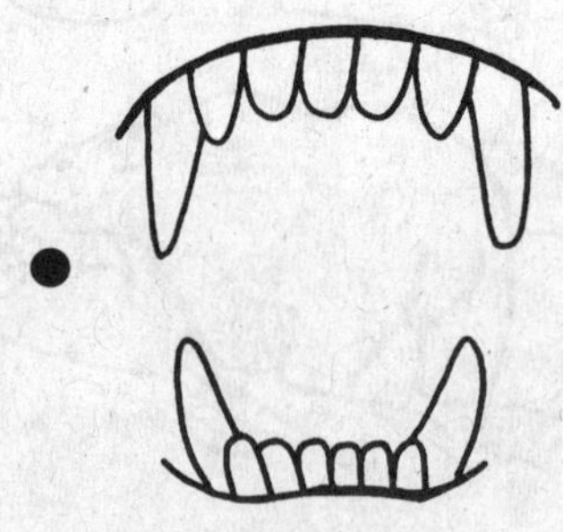

3.

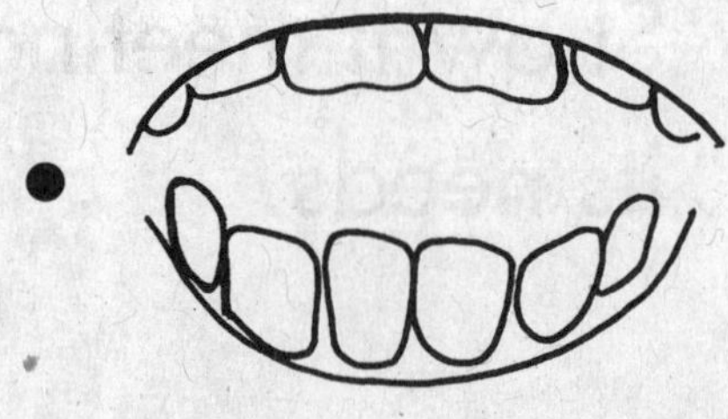

Harcourt

Use with page A47.

Name ______________________

Science Skills Practice

Classify

Match each animal to its body covering.

1. mammal •

2. bird •

3. reptile •

4. amphibian •

5. fish •

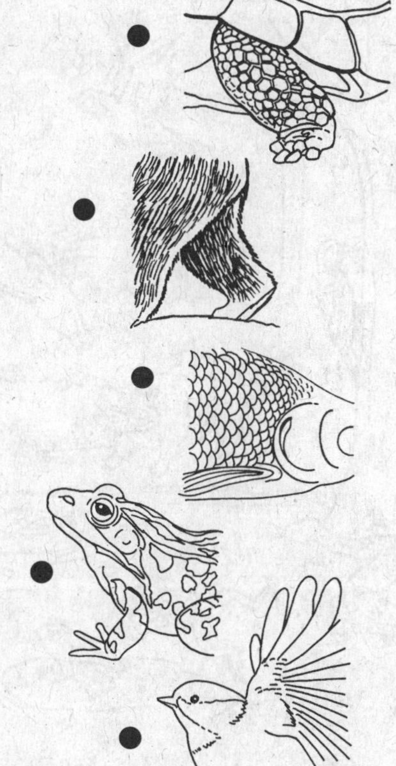

6. Write the name or draw a picture of an animal in each group.

Mammal	Bird	Reptile

Name ________________________________

What Are Some Kinds of Animals?

Many kinds of animals live in this forest.

1. Color all the amphibians **orange**.

2. Color all the mammals **brown**.

3. Color all the reptiles **green**.

4. Color all the birds **blue**.

5. Another kind of animal is also in the picture. Write its name.

____

Use with page A53.

Name ______________________________

Make a Model

1. Draw the parts so they make an insect.

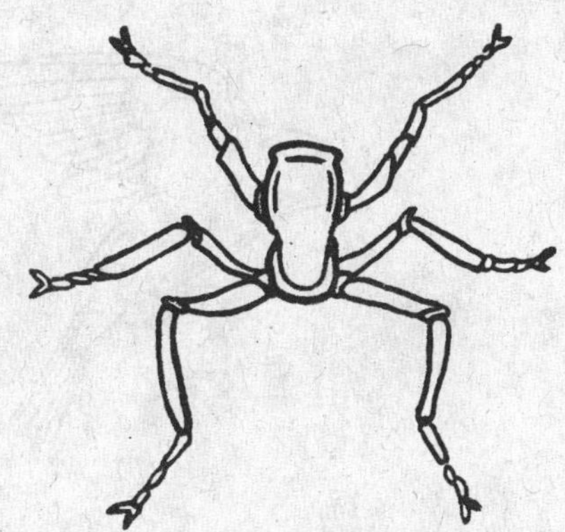

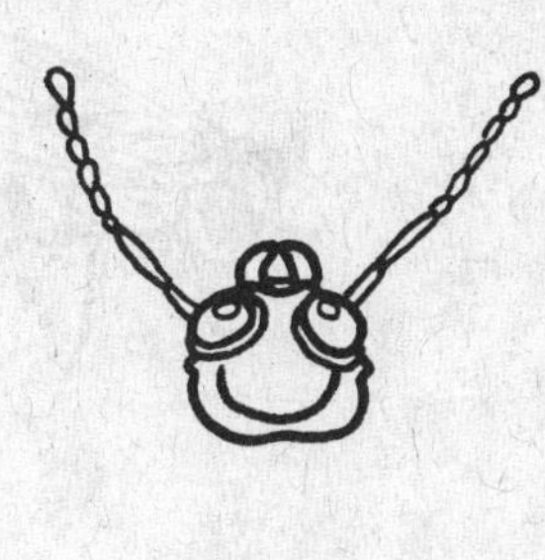

2. Name this insect.

____

Name ___________________________

What Are Insects?

1. Color the animals that are insects.

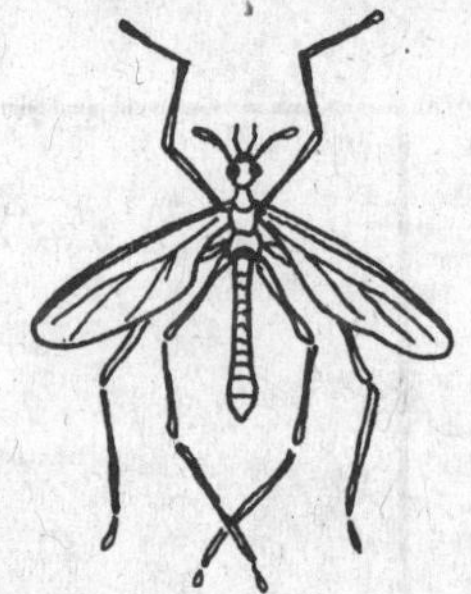

2. How many body parts does an insect have? ______________

3. How many legs does an insect have? ______________

4. Draw two kinds of insects. Draw one with wings.

Use with page A57.

Name ________________________________

Compare

1. Compare the animals.

	Ways they are the same.	**Ways they are different.**
swan		
dog		

2. Circle the part that shows how these animals are helping their young.

Use with page A58.

Name ______________________

How Do Animals Grow?

Match the animal to where it came from.

1. 

2. 

3. 

4. 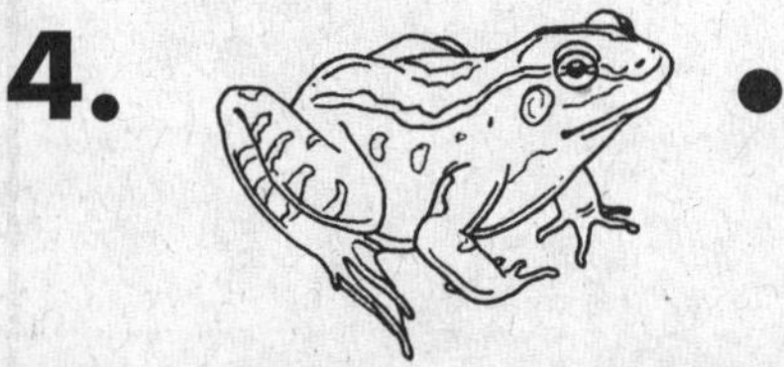

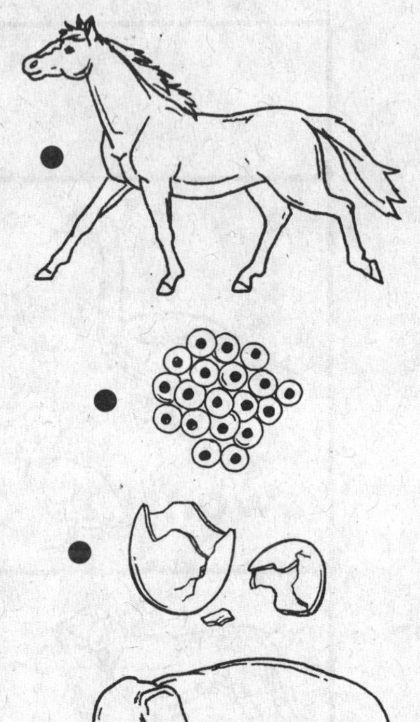

5. What are two things an animal can teach its young?

____

____

____

Use with page A63.

Name ______________________________

Observe

1. Color the butterflies **red**.
2. Color the larva **blue**.
3. Color the pupa **yellow**.
4. From what does a caterpillar hatch?

   ____

5. What comes out of a pupa?

   ____

Name ____________________

How Does a Butterfly Grow?

Draw a line under the best ending.

1. A caterpillar hatches from an egg. The caterpillar becomes a pupa and makes a hard covering. The pupa changes into a ____.

larva   butterfly   bigger caterpillar

2. These butterflies live in a field of flowers. They keep safe by hiding. Color the flowers and the butterflies. Help the butterflies hide.

Use with page A69.

Name ______________________

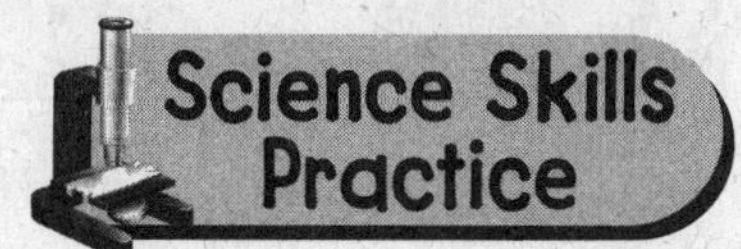

Sequence

1. Tell how the frog grows after it hatches. Write **first**, **next**, or **last** next to each picture.

____

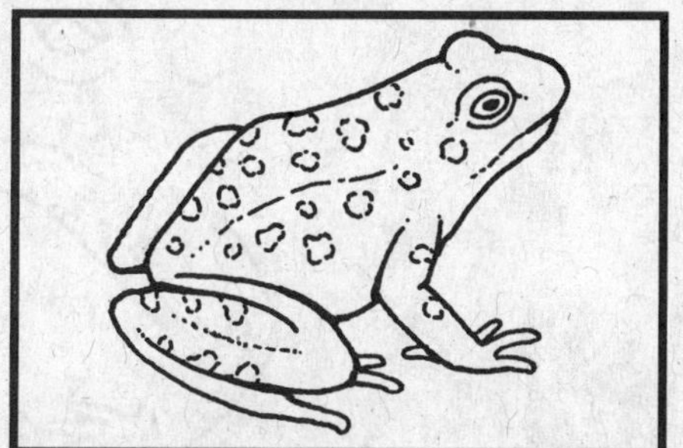

____

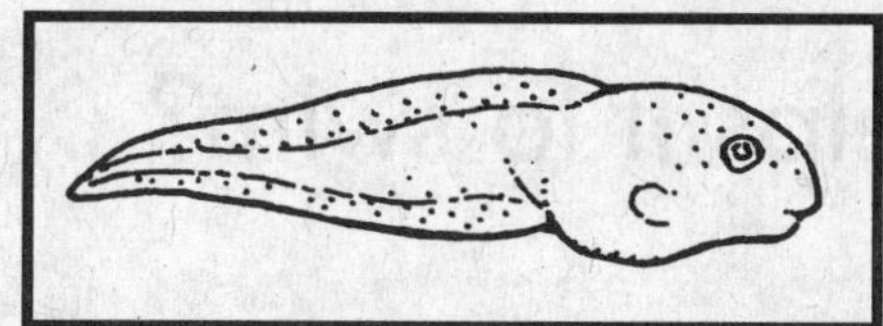

____

2. Read the sentences. Number them in sequence. The first one is done for you.

______ Young frogs climb onto land.

______ Tadpoles use their tails to swim.

__1__ Frogs lay eggs in the water.

______ Tadpoles hatch from the eggs.

Name ____________________

How Does a Frog Grow?

1. Finish each drawing.

tadpole

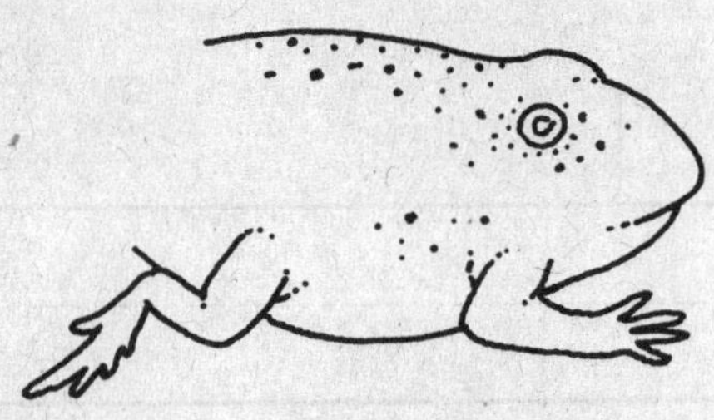

frog

2. What part of the tadpole helps it to swim? Color that part **red**.

3. Draw where a frog will lay its eggs.

Harcourt

Use with page A73.

Name ______________________________

All About Animals

1. What kind of animal is it? Draw a line to match.

amphibian insect reptile mammal

Finish the sentences. Use the words in the box.

hatch	larva	pupa

2. When chicks break out of eggs, they ______________.

3. A tiny caterpillar is called a ______________.

4. A caterpillar makes a hard covering called a ______________.

Name ____________________

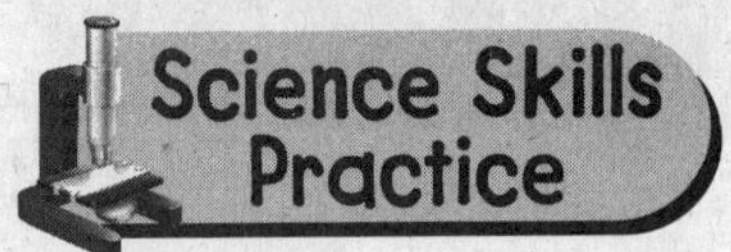

Observe

Animals use plants for different things.

1. Color the plants used for food **green**.
2. One animal uses a plant to make a nest.
   Color the nest **yellow**.
3. Color the plants used for shelter **brown**.
4. One animal uses plants to hide.
   Tell about that animal.

____

____

Use with page B4.

Name ____________________

How Do Animals Need Plants?

1. Match each animal to how it is using plants.

• • shelter

• • food

2. Finish the drawing. Show how an animal uses a log for shelter and food.

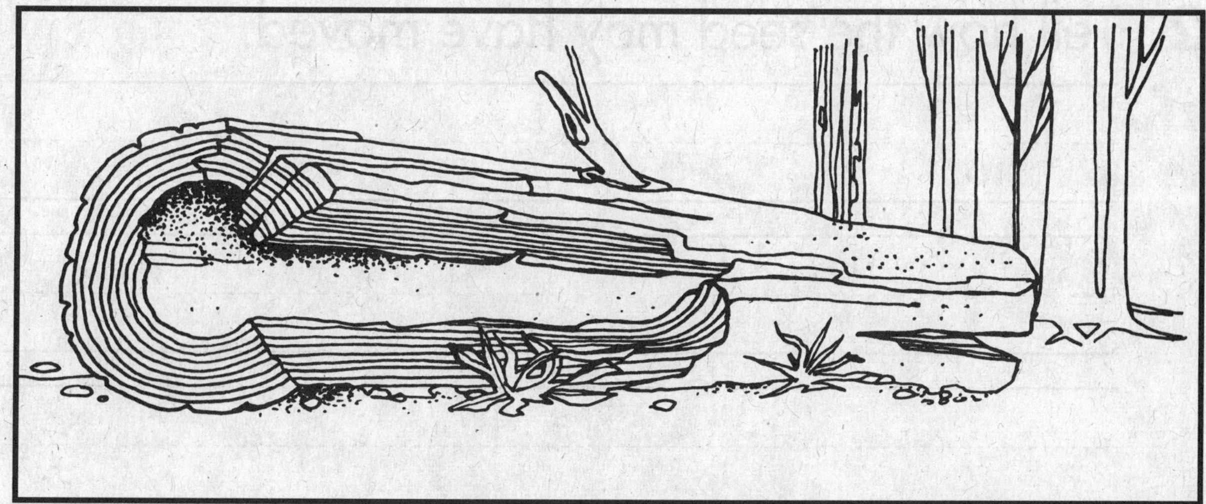

Name ______________________________

Investigate

A plant grew in Jason's yard. A plant just like it grew in Sara's yard. Sara and Jason investigate how a seed was carried to Sara's yard.

1. Circle what you think moved the seed from one yard to the other.

2. Tell how the seed may have moved.

____

____

____

____

Use with page B10.

Name ______________________

How Do Animals Help Plants?

1. Circle the animals that are helping plants.

2. Tell how a butterfly helps a flower. Write or draw.

Name ______________________________

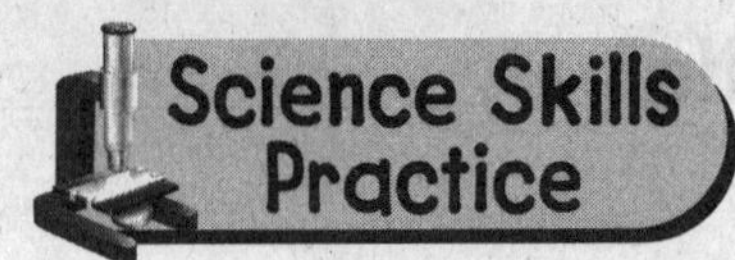

Classify

Circle the things made from plants. Mark an **X** on the things made from animals.

1.

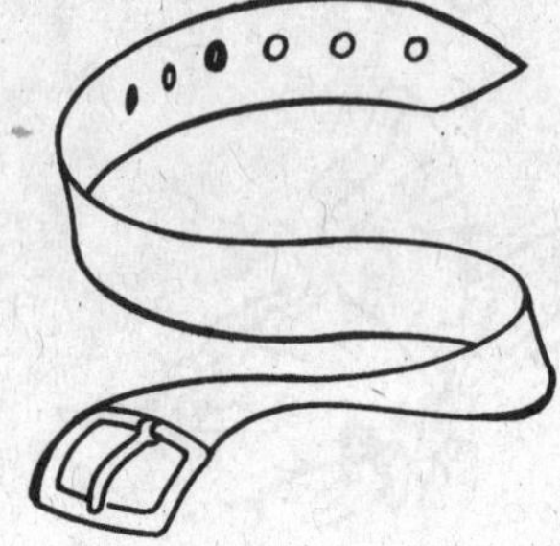

2.

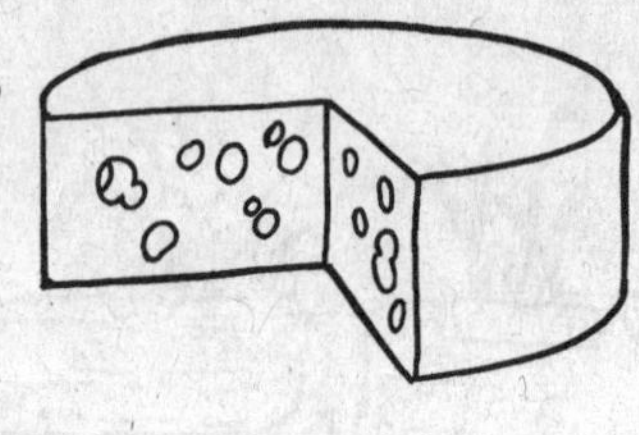

3.

4.

5.

6.

7.

8.

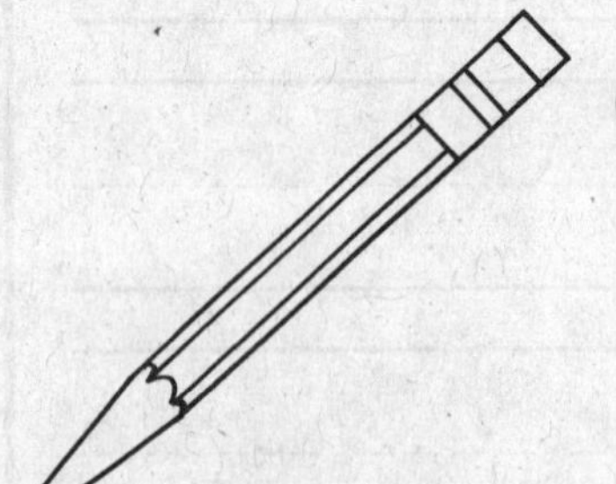

9.

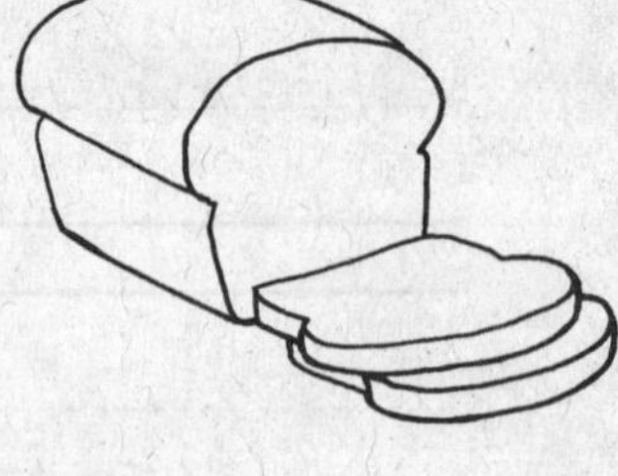

Use with page B14.

Name ______________________________

How Do We Need Plants and Animals?

Match each product to the animal or plant it came from.

1.  • • 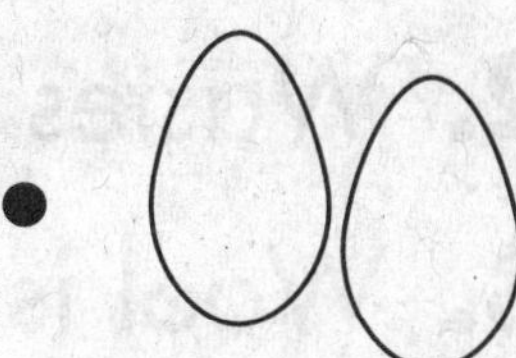

2.  • • 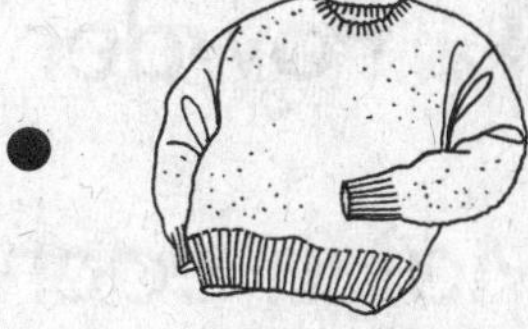

3.  • • 

4.  • • 

5. Tell how an animal can be a helper to a person. Write or draw.

____

____

____

Name ____________________

Plants and Animals Need One Another

Draw a line under each sentence that is true.

1. Animals use shelter for food.
2. Wastes can help enrich soil.
3. Wool is an animal product used for clothing.
4. Powder from flowers is called pollen.

Match each word to the correct picture.

5. shelter • 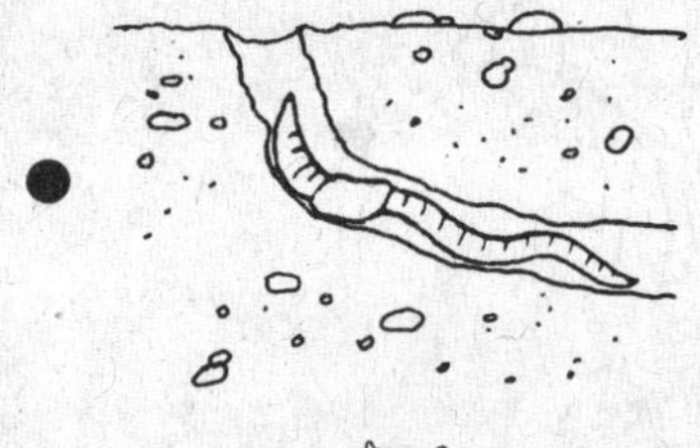

6. enrich • 

7. product • 

8. pollen • 

 Use with pages B22–B23.

Name ______________________

Compare

1. Tell how these leaves are the same.

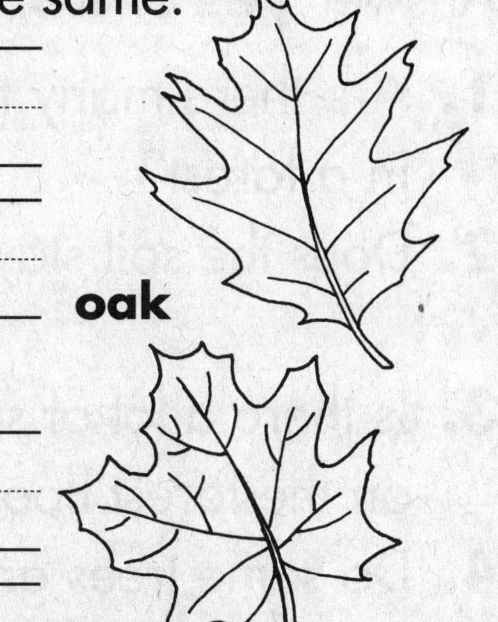

oak

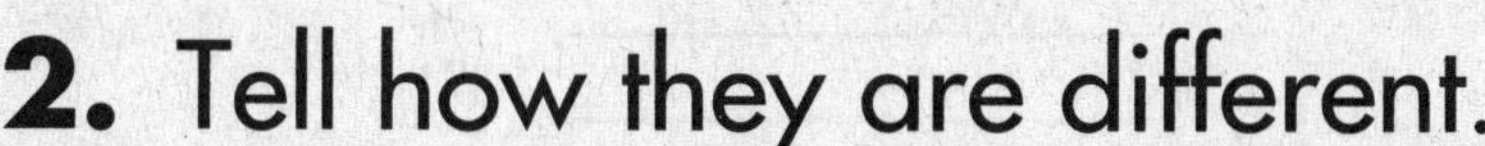

2. Tell how they are different.

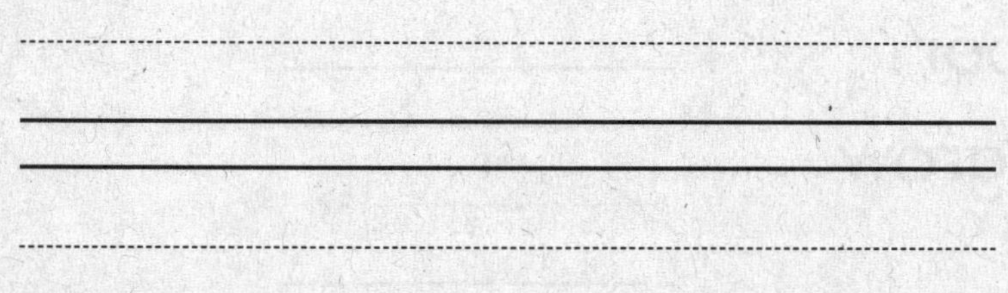

maple

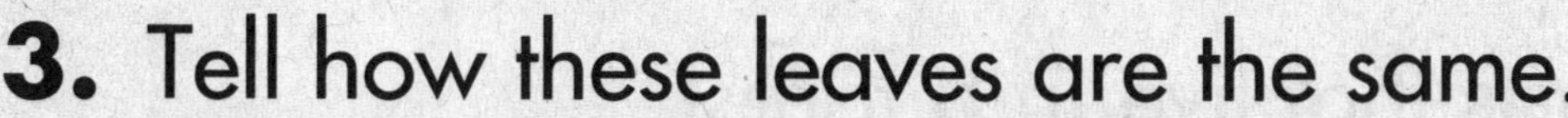

3. Tell how these leaves are the same.

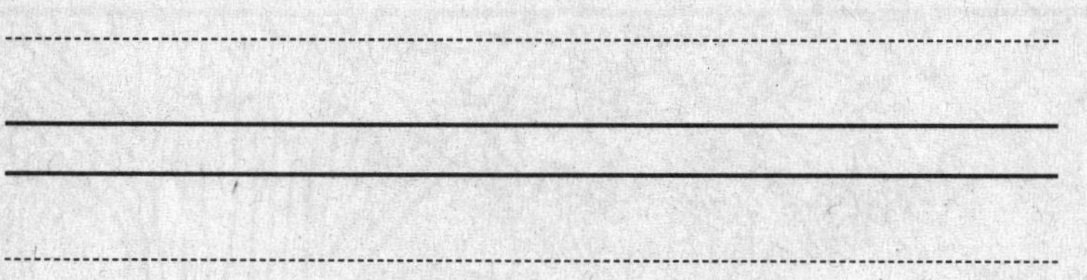

rose

4. Tell how they are different.

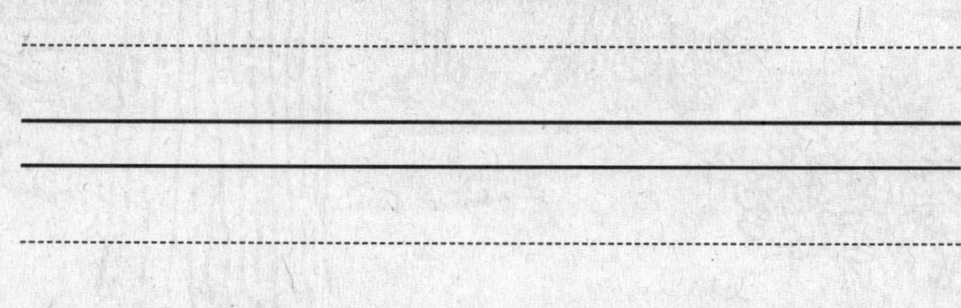

ivy

Name ____________________

What Lives in a Forest?

Answer **yes** or **no**.

1. Are there many trees in a forest? ____________

2. Does the soil stay dry? ____________

3. Is there a lot of sunlight on the forest floor? ____________

4. Do some trees grow tall in a forest? ____________

5. Finish the picture of the forest. Show plants and animals that live in a forest.

Name ______________________________

Science Skills Practice

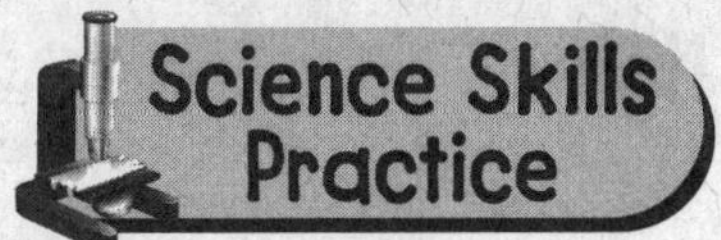

Draw a Conclusion

These animals live in a desert. Put an **X** where an animal might go to stay cool in the daytime. Color the picture.

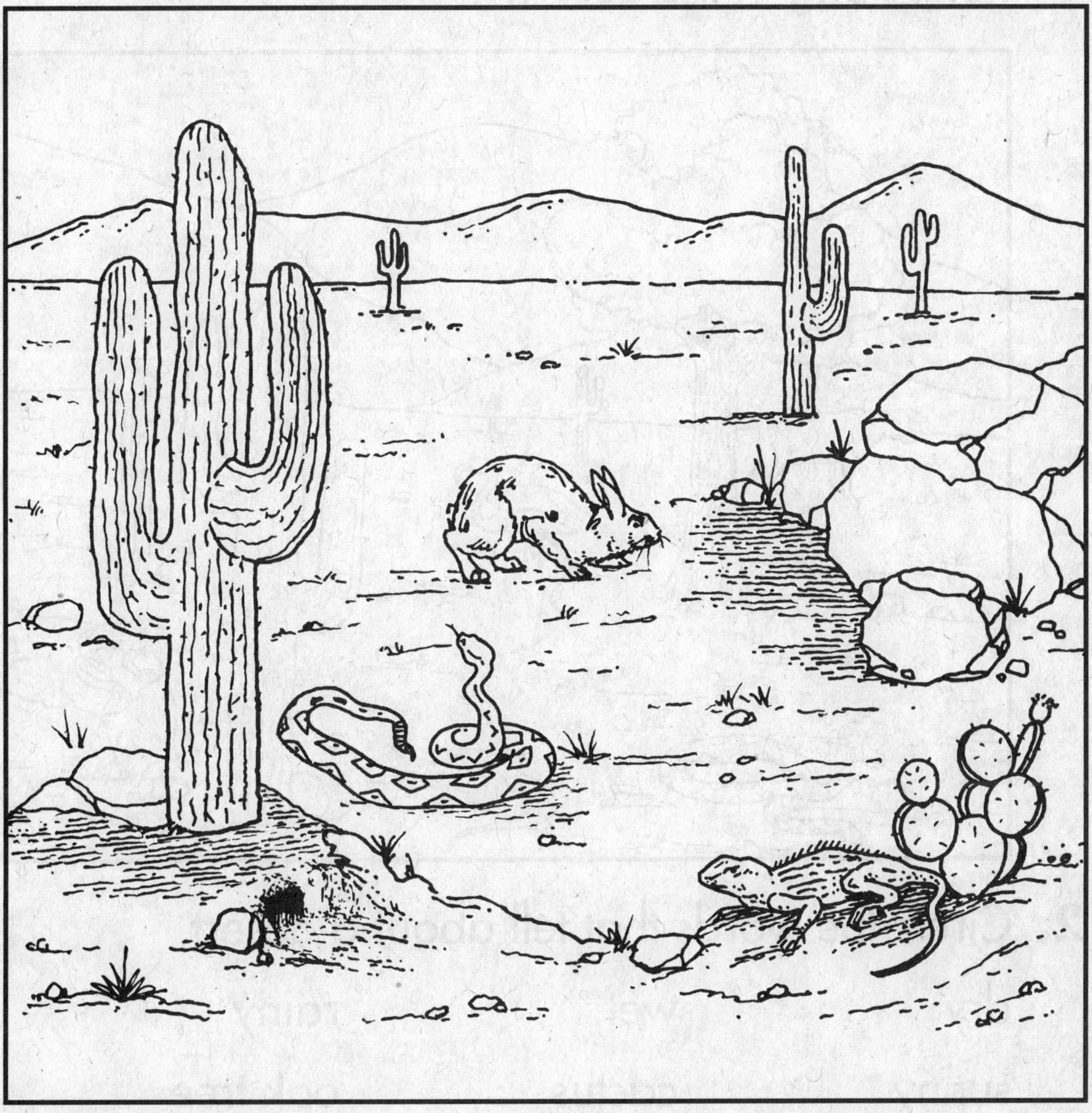

Name ______________________

What Lives in the Desert?

1. Mark an **X** on the plants and animals that do not belong in the desert.

2. Circle the words that tell about a desert.

dry	wet	rainy
sunny	cactus	oak tree

Use with page B33.

Name ______________________

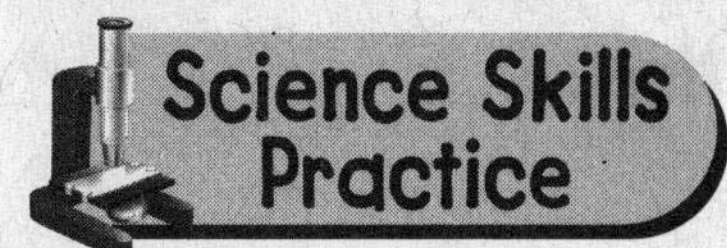

Communicate

1. Tell about plants that grow where there is little light. Write or draw.

2. Tell about plants that grow where there is a lot of light. Write or draw.

Name ______________________________

What Lives in a Rain Forest?

1. Draw animals that live at each level of the rain forest.

Draw a line under the best answer.

2. Most rain forests are _____.
cool and dry   wet and warm   wet and cool

3. Plants that need a lot of light live at the _____ of the rain forest.
bottom   middle   top

 Use with page B37.

Name ______________________________

Classify

Color the animals that live in the ocean. Mark **X** through the animals that do **not** live in the ocean.

1.

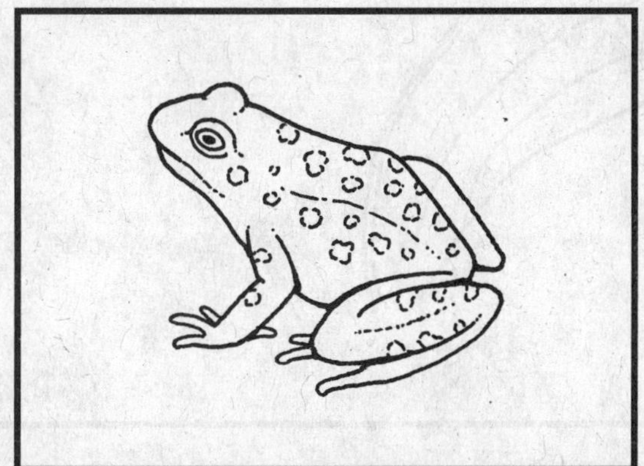

2.

3.

4.

5.

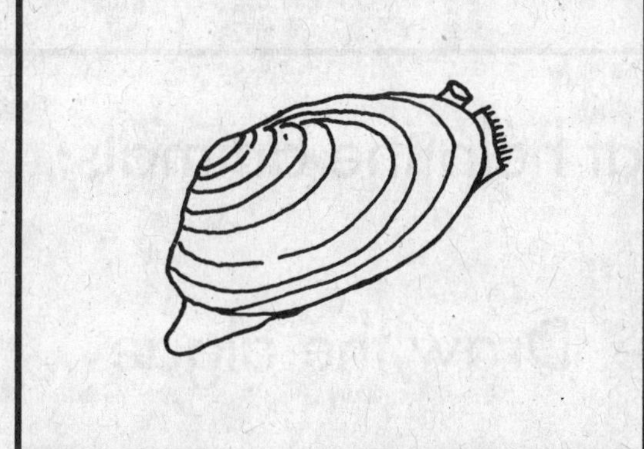

6.

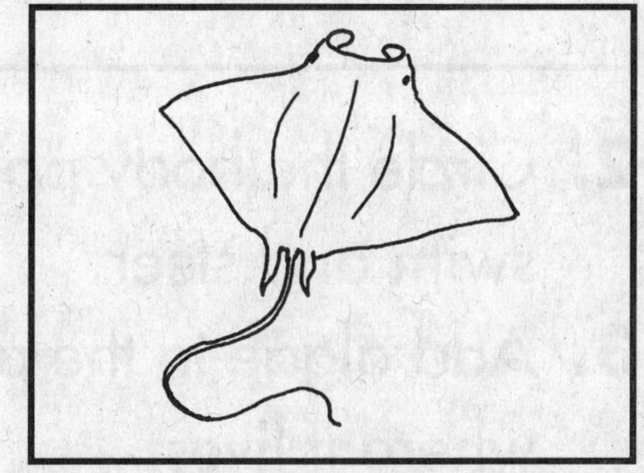

Name ______________________

What Lives in the Ocean?

1. Complete the picture. Show what helps the animal swim fast to catch food.

2. Circle the body parts that help the animals swim and steer.
3. Add algae to the picture. Draw the algae where it lives.

 Use with page B41.

Name ______________________

A Place to Live

Label each picture. Use the words in the box.

algae	desert	forest	ocean	rain forest

1. ______________________

2. ______________________

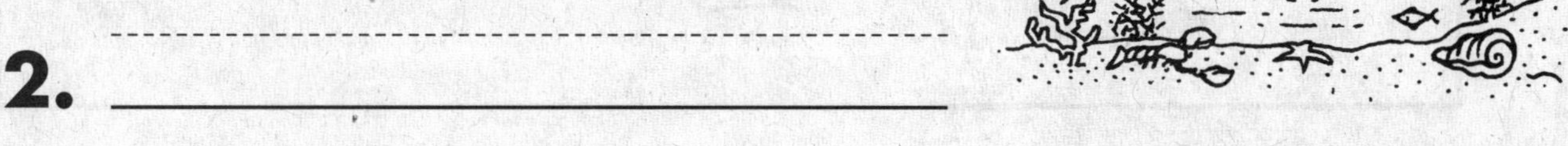

3. ______________________

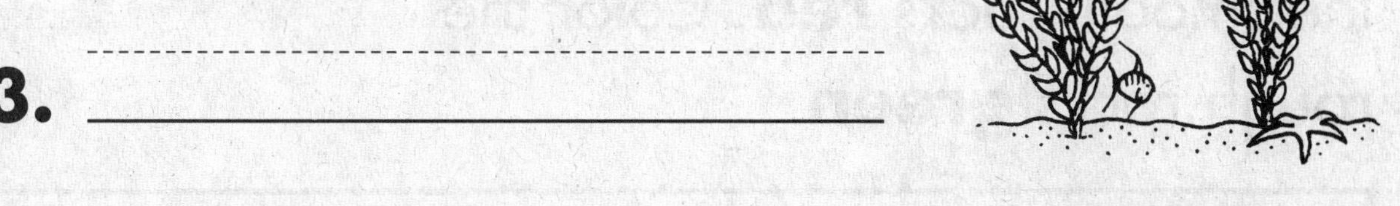

4. ______________________

5. ______________________

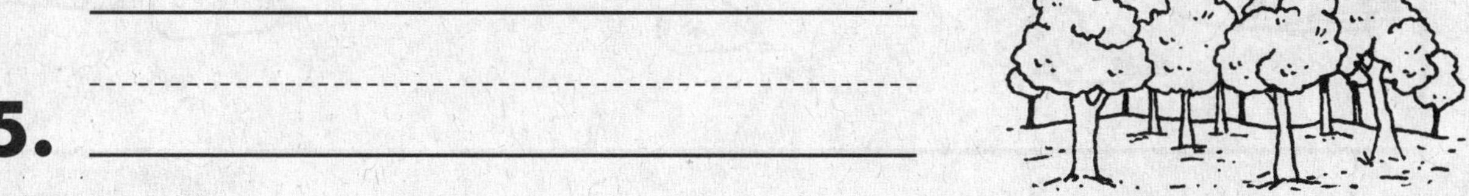

Use with pages B44–B45.

Name ________________________________

Classify

1. Classify the rocks. Color the large rocks **yellow**. Color the small rocks **blue**.

2. Classify the rocks another way. Color the smooth rocks **red**. Color the rough rocks **green**.

Use with page C4.

Name ______________________________

What Can We Observe About Rocks?

1. Color the rocks **red**. Color the sand **yellow**.

2. People use rocks in different ways. Draw a picture that shows one way people use rocks.

Name ______________________________

Observe

Write two things found in soil.

1. ____________________ 2. ____________________

3. Circle the senses that help you observe soil.

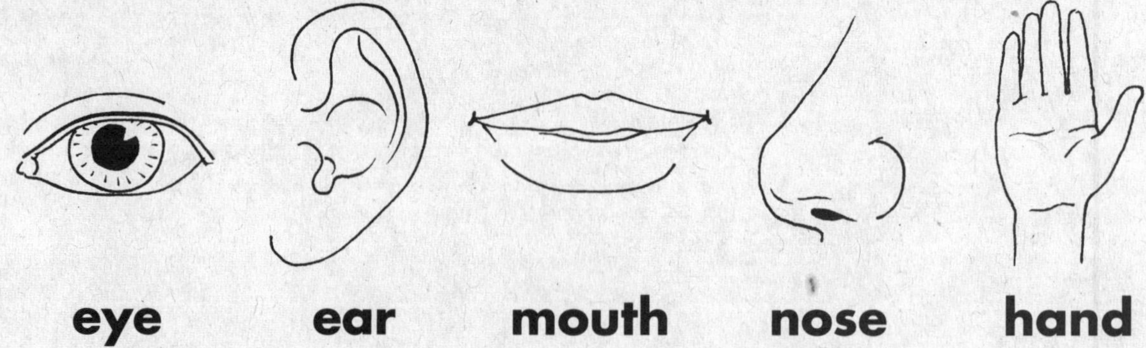

eye ear mouth nose hand

Use with page C8.

Name ___________________________

What Is Soil?

Tell how each person uses soil.

1. ___________________________

2. ___________________________

3. Draw what else you might see in soil.

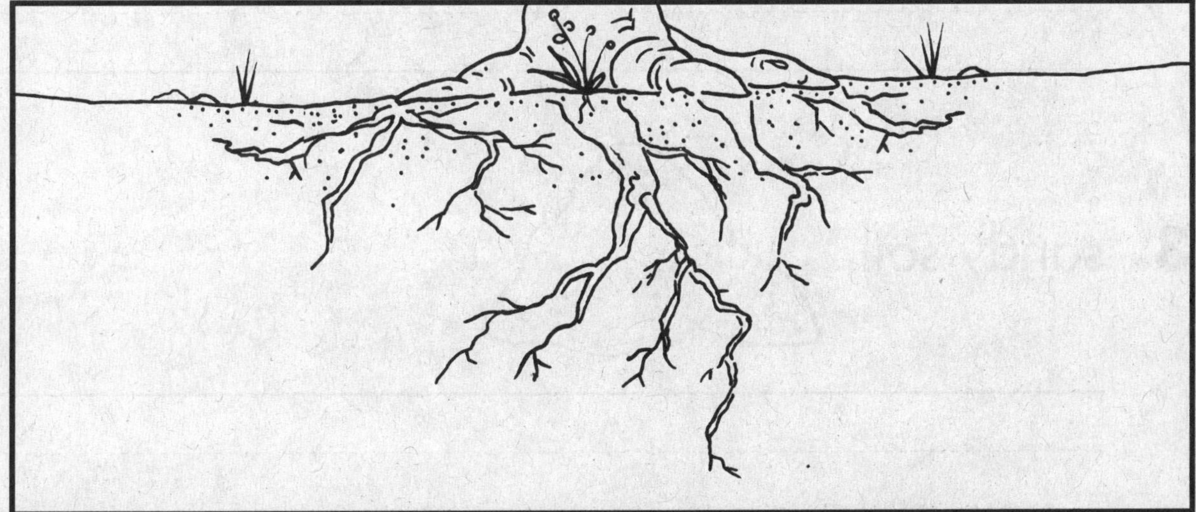

Name ______________________

Compare

Describe each soil. Use the words in the box.

sticky	rough	has bits of dead plants in it

1. topsoil

____

____

2. clay soil

____

____

3. sandy soil

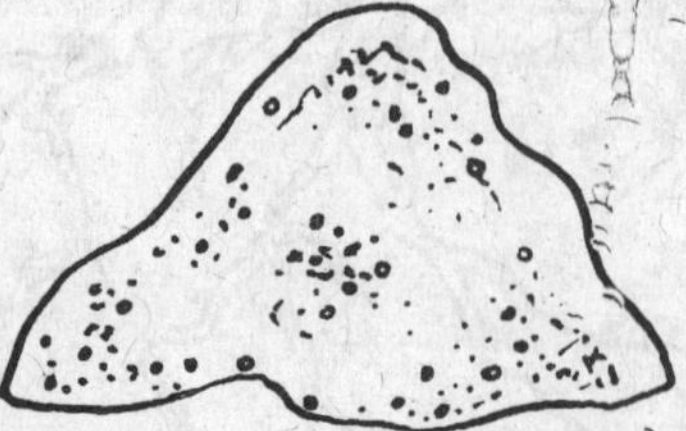

____

____

Use with page C12.

Name ______________________________

How Do Different Soils Compare?

1. Color the topsoil **brown**. Color the clay soil **red**. Color the sandy soil **yellow**.

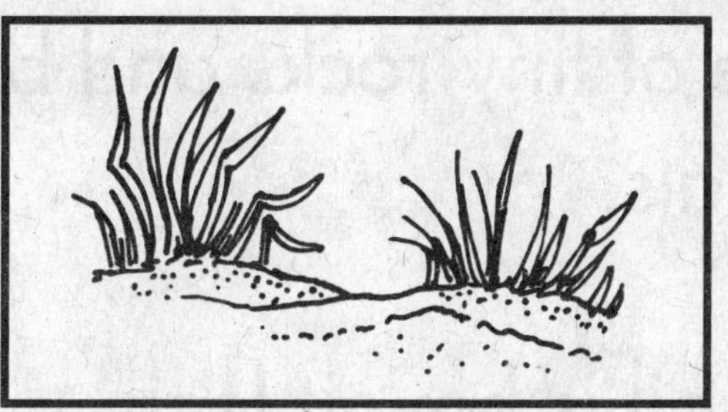

- sticky
- dark
- sandy

2. Match each picture to a word that tells about it.

3. Circle the soil that can hold the most water.

Name ______________________

Earth's Land

Write a word to fill in each blank.

sand	rock	soil	texture

1. ______________ is made of tiny rocks and bits of dead plants and animals.

2. The ______________ of soil is how it feels.

3. Tiny pieces of rock are called ______________.

4. A ______________ is a hard, nonliving thing that comes from the Earth.

Write a sentence about the picture. Underline the word that names the picture.

5. ____

Use with pages C18–C19.

Name ___________________________

Infer

Air is all around. You can not see air. But you can see what it does.

1. Circle in the picture the things that air is moving.
2. Put an **X** on something filled with air.
3. Color all the living things. They use air, too.

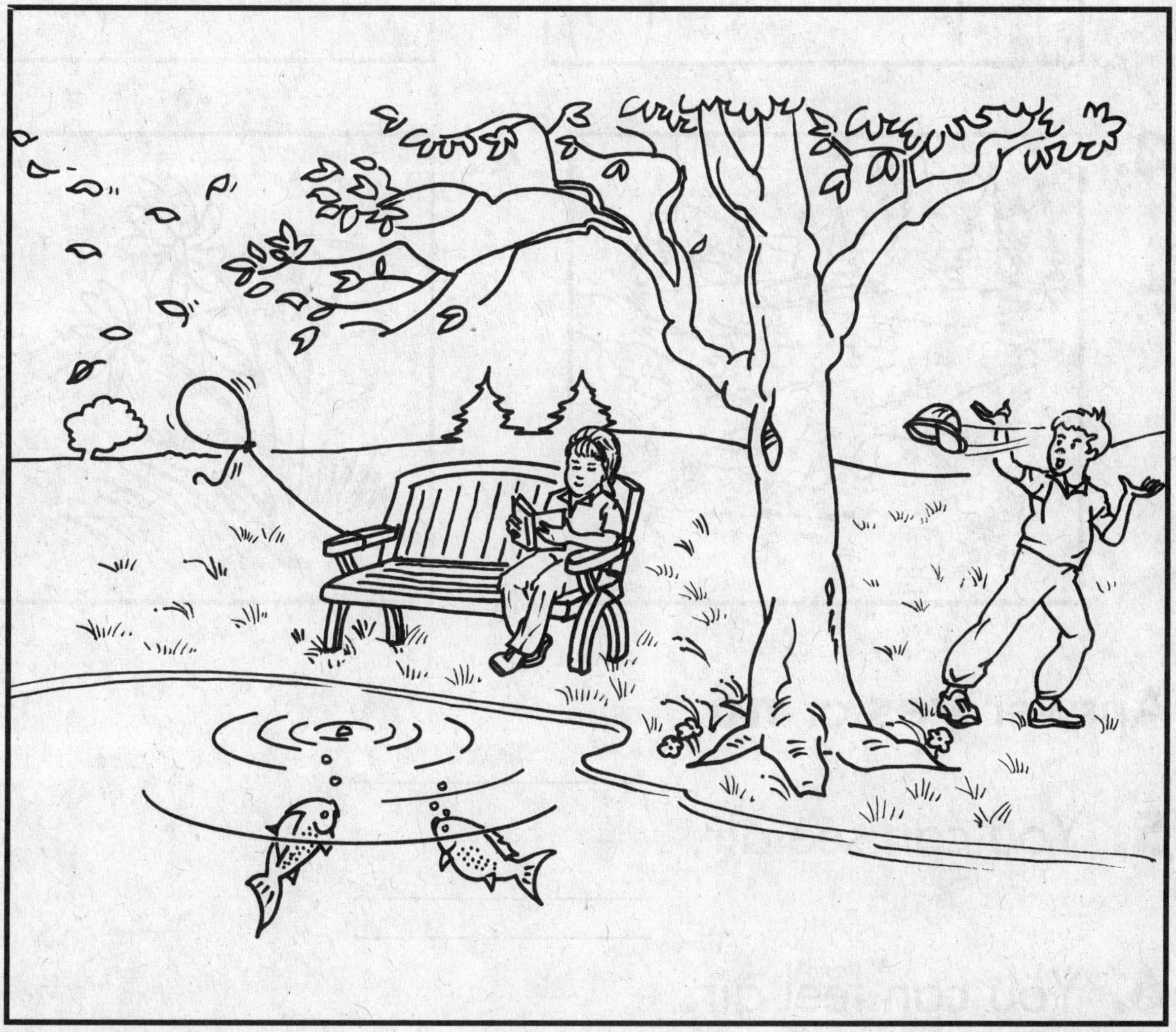

Name ______________________________

Where Is Air on Earth?

Color where the air is in each picture.

1.

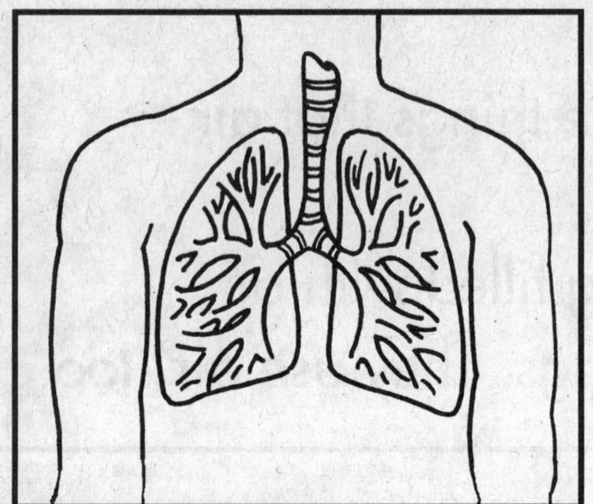

2.

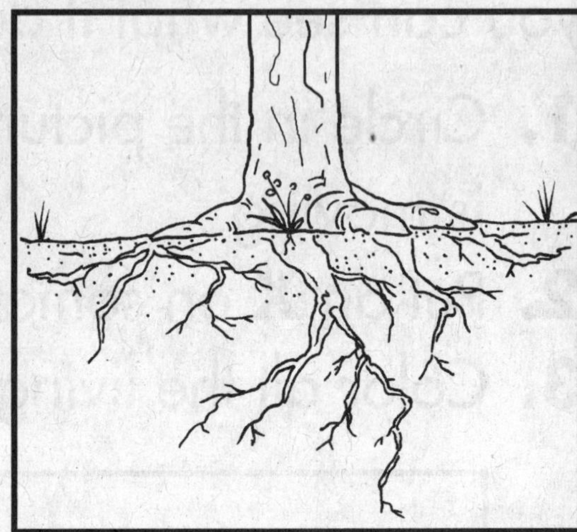

3.

4.

Answer **yes** or **no**.

5. You can see air. ______________

6. You can feel air. ______________

Name ______________________

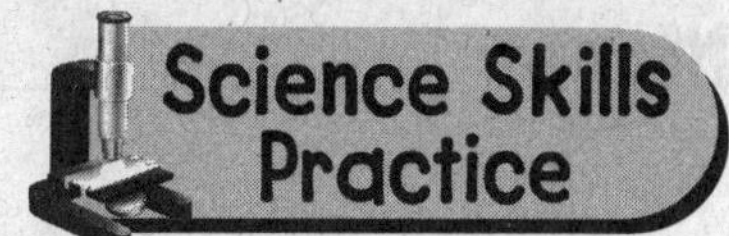

Draw a Conclusion

The ocean has salt water. Snow and rain are fresh water.

1. Color the fresh water **blue**.

2. Color the salt water **green**.

3. Tell how you use fresh water.

____

____

____

Name ______________________________

Where Is Fresh Water Found?

Match to tell how people use fresh water.

1.

• cooking

2.

• washing

• drinking

3.

4. Draw a freshwater lake. Color it **blue**.

Use with page C29.

Name ___________________________

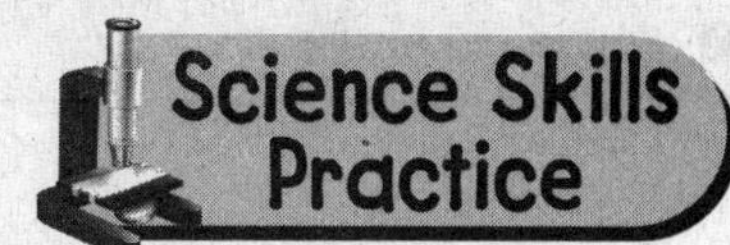

Communicate

1. What senses can you use to tell about salt water? Circle the words.

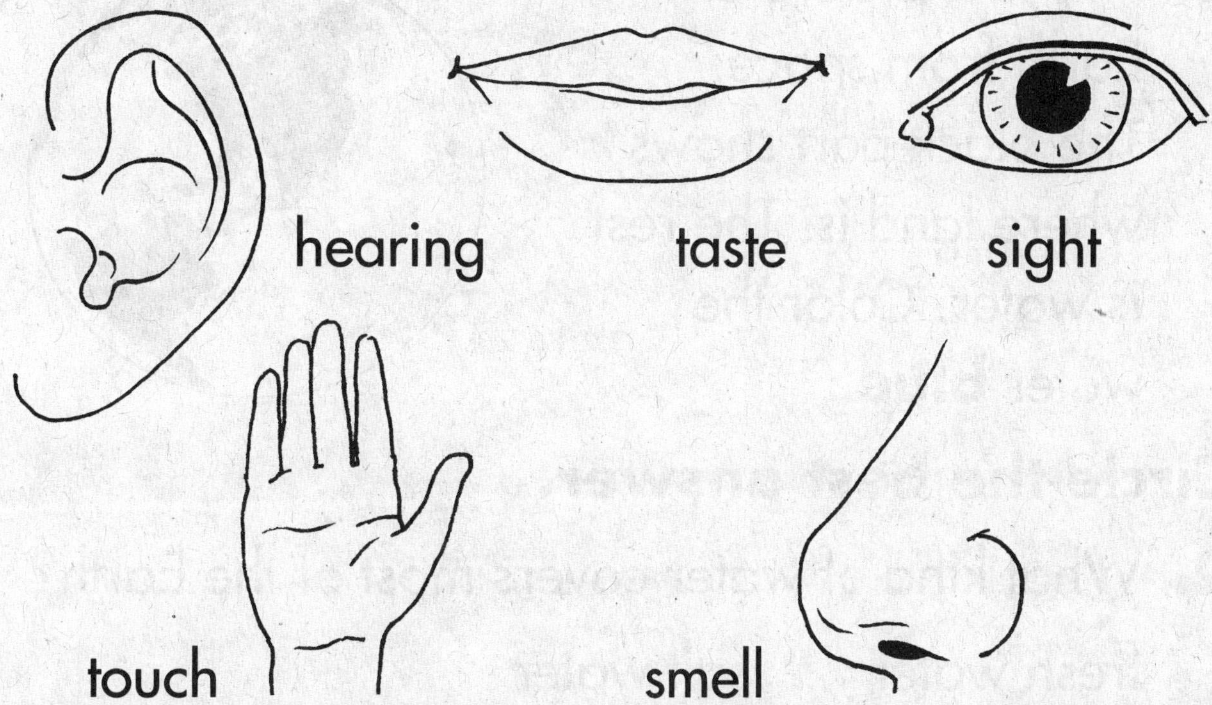

2. Write a sentence. Tell how you can use sea salt.

____

____

____

____

Name ______________________________

Where Is Salt Water on Earth?

1. This is a picture of Earth from space. The black part shows where land is. The rest is water. Color the water **blue**.

Circle the best answer.

2. What kind of water covers most of the Earth?

fresh water salt water

3. Where is most of this water found?

rivers oceans lakes

4. How can people safely drink salt water?

They drink it with the salt in it.

They take the salt out of the water.

People never drink salt water.

Use with page C33.

Name ______________________

Earth's Air and Water

1. Color the fresh water **blue**. Color the salt water **green**. Circle the **river**.

Write your answer. Use the words in the box.

stream	air	lake

2. You can't see me, smell me, or taste me. I am all around you. What am I? ______________________

3. I am a body of fresh water. There is land all around me. What am I? ______________________

4. I am flowing water. What am I? ______________________

Name ______________________________

Compare

1. Tell how the pictures are the same and different. Write your answers in the chart.

My Chart	
Same	**Different**

2. Color the picture that shows sunny weather.

Use with page D4.

Name ______________________________

Infer

1. Juan would like to grow beans. Color the picture that shows the best time to plant the seeds.

2. Tell why you colored that picture.

____

____

____

3. Circle the words that tell about what a seed needs to begin to grow.

water warmth light air

Name ____________________

What Is Spring?

1. Circle the things that are found in spring.

2. Circle the words that best finish the sentence.

Spring has _____.

cooler air   falling leaves   more hours of daylight

3. Draw how growing plants help young animals.

Use with page D29.

Name ______________________

Order

1. Write the temperatures from coolest to hottest.

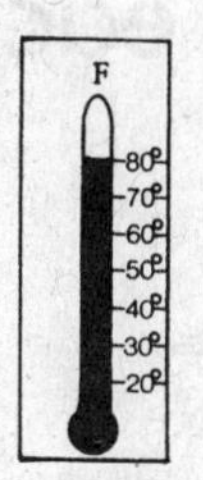

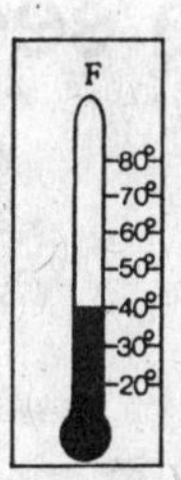

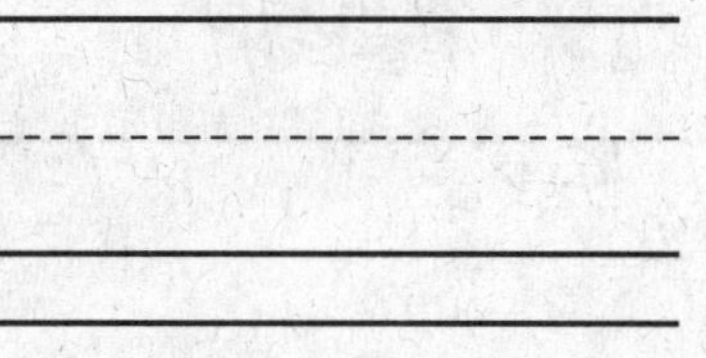

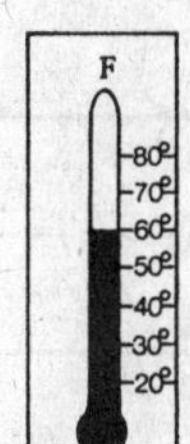

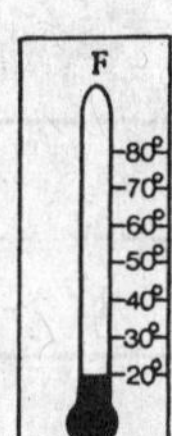

2. These words tell how a plant will grow. Draw pictures to show how a plant will grow.

seed

sprout

flower

Use with page D30.

Name ______________________

What Is Summer?

Animals look different in spring and summer.
Tell which season each picture shows.

1. ______________________

2. ______________________

3. ______________________

4. ______________________

5. Draw flowers and trees in summer.

Use with page D33.

Name ______________________

Science Skills Practice

Predict

1. Draw what these trees will look like when they have fruit ready for picking. Color the fruit on each tree.

orange tree

cherry tree

2. In spring, this kitten was born. In summer, it grew. Draw what the kitten will look like next.

Name ______________________

What Is Fall?

Circle the answer that fits the sentence best.

1. The season that follows summer is _____ .

spring fall

2. In fall there are _____ hours of daylight.

less more

3. In some places, leaves change in fall. Draw one of those places. Color it.

4. It is fall. Tell what this animal is doing.

Harcourt

Name ______________________________

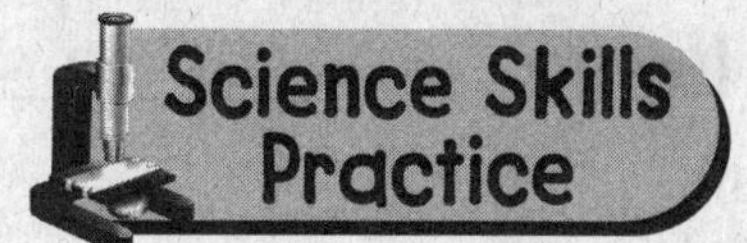

Investigate

1. Circle the gloves that are best for keeping warm.

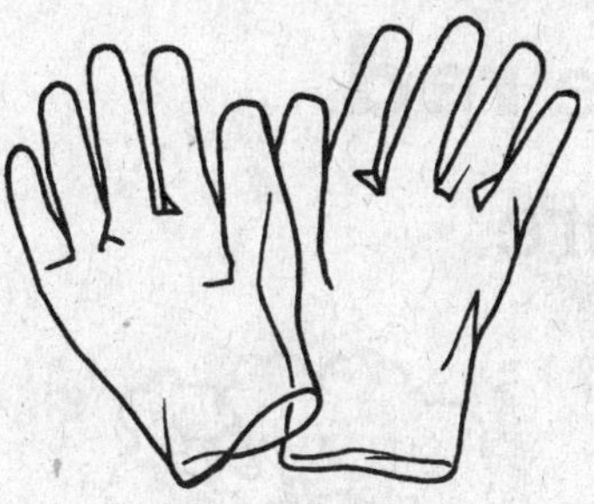

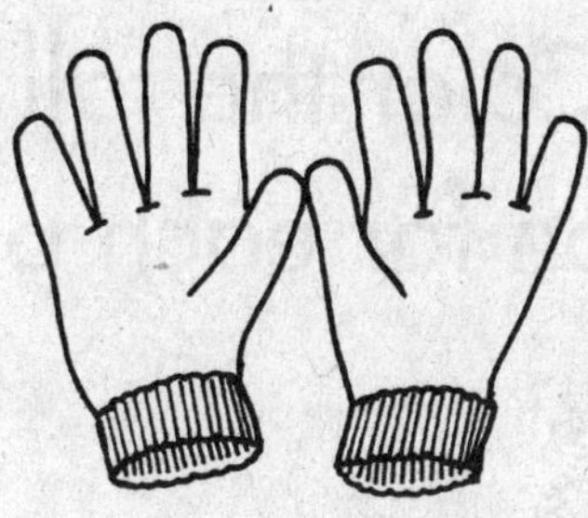

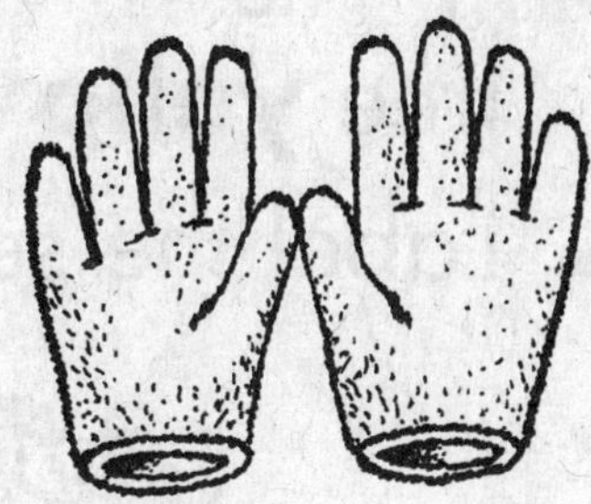

2. Carol has a pair of boots. One boot has a hole. Tell how Carol could investigate which boot has a hole. Draw pictures of the things she could use to help.

Name ___________________________

What Is Winter?

1. Color the winter tree **blue**. Color the spring tree **green**. Color the summer tree **yellow**. Color the fall tree **red**. Label the season for each picture.

2. Tell what a plant might look like in winter.

Harcourt

Use with page D41.

Name ______________________

The Seasons

Label each picture. Use the words in the box.

spring	summer	fall	winter

1. ______________________

2. ______________________

3. ______________________

4. ______________________

These sentences are **false**. Change the underlined word to make the sentences **true**.

5. In <u>spring</u>, leaves drop from the trees. ______________________

6. There is less daylight in <u>summer</u>. ______________________

Name ___________________________

Classify

1. Group the objects that are the same. Draw your groups in the chart.

My Groups	
Group 1	**Group 2**

2. Tell why you grouped the objects as you did.

____

____

Use with page E4.

Name ______________________

What Can We Observe About Solids?

1. Draw something that is matter.

2. Color the solids **red**.

3. How is this man changing a solid?

____

____

Harcourt

Name ______________________

Use Numbers

1. Circle the container you think has more water.

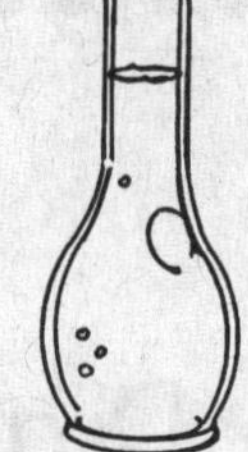

A B

2. Circle the tool you could use to measure the water.

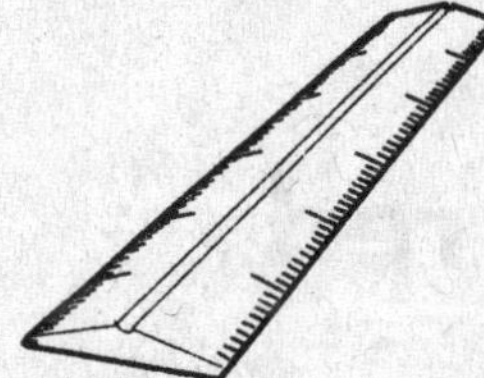
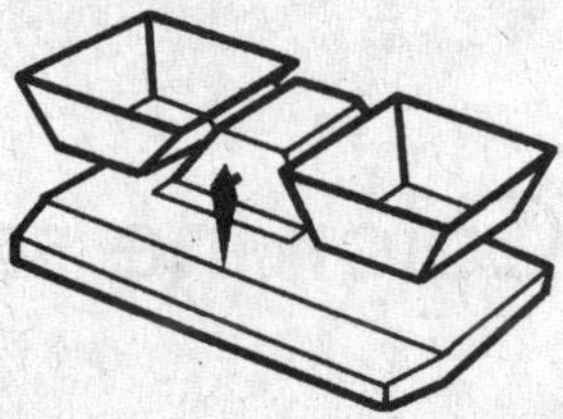

3. Jill measured the water in each container. Both containers had 12 ounces. Circle the words that tell about the containers.

Container A ____.

a. has more water than Container B

b. has the same amount of water as Container B

c. has less water than Container B

4. Why does B look as if it has more water than A?

____

____

 Use with page E8.

Name ___________________________

What Can We Observe About Liquids?

1. Draw liquids in the containers.

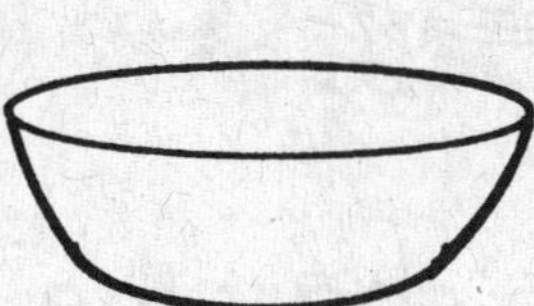

2. What if both bottles tip over? Circle the liquid that would run out faster. Tell why.

____

____

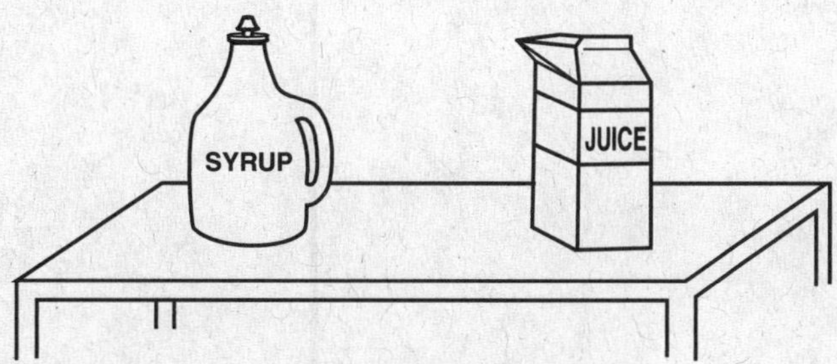

3. Circle the things that are liquid.

Name ______________________

Gather and Record Data

1. Observe the picture. Record in the chart the liquids and solids.

Matter	
Liquids	**Solids**

2. How many solids are there? ______________

3. How many liquids are there? ______________

Use with page E12.

Name ________________________________

What Objects Sink or Float?

Circle **float** or **sink** for each picture.

1. 

float sink

2. 

float sink

3. 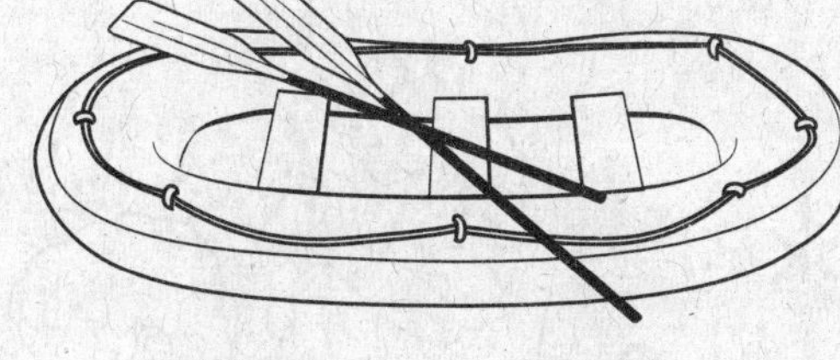

float sink

4. 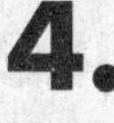 

float sink

5. Draw something that floats and something that sinks. Color the object that floats **red**. Color the object that sinks **blue**.

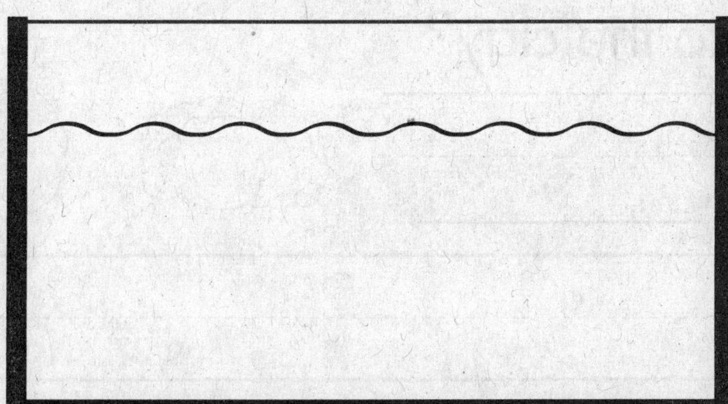

Name ______________________________

Draw a Conclusion

1. These spoons had different liquids on them. Why is one liquid still on the spoon?

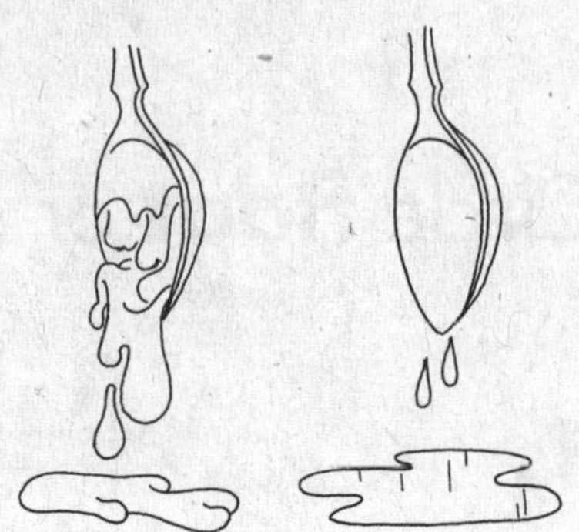

2. The boy has the same balloon in both pictures. Why does the balloon look different in the second picture?

3. What happened to the clay?

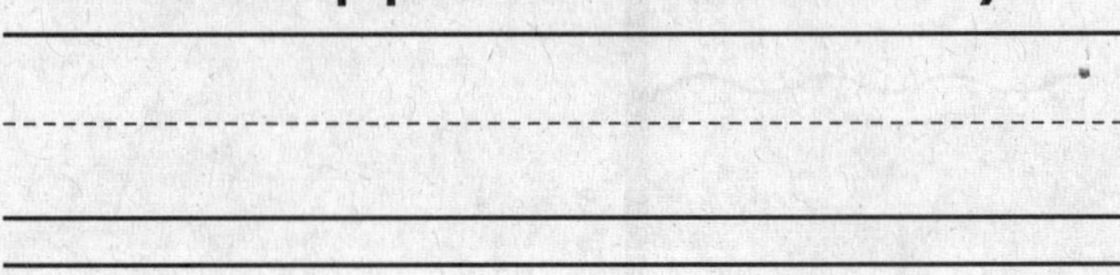

Use with page E16.

Name ______________________

What Can We Observe About Gases?

1. There is gas in each container. Color the space the gas takes up.

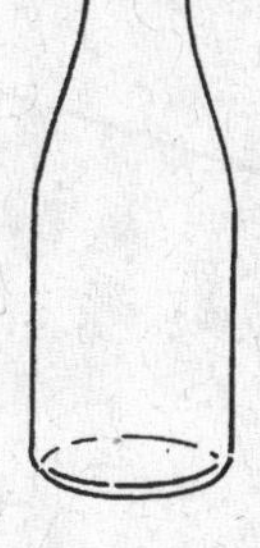

2. Color where the gas is in this liquid.

3. You can not see air.
How do you know it is here?

____

____

Harcourt

Name ______________________

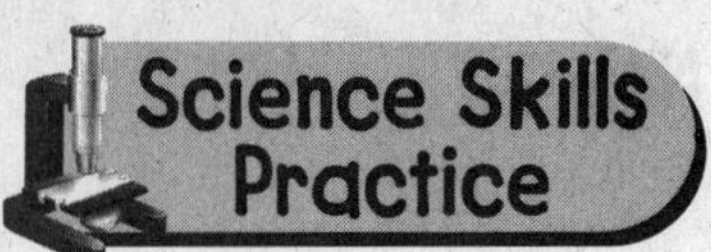

Investigate

1. These pictures are not finished. Finish each picture a different way.

2. These pictures are the same. Color each picture to make it look different.

Use with page E20.

Name ______________________________

How Can We Change Objects?

1. This toy is made of wire. Draw how you could bend it to make it look different.

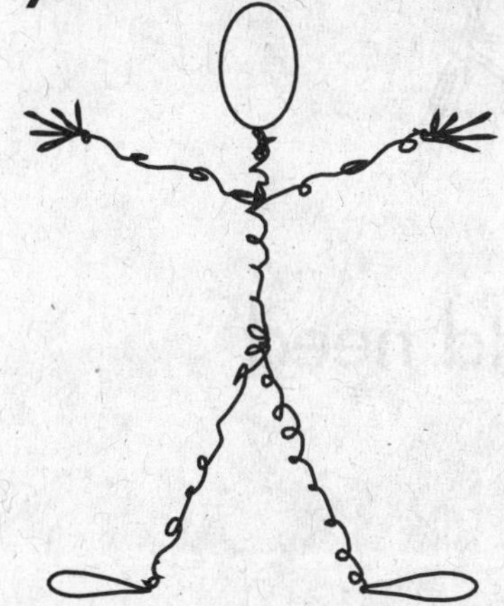

2. You could change this paper with scissors. Draw how it would look after you cut it.

3. Finish the sentence. Circle the best word.

_____ changes liquid juice to a frozen ice pop.

Melting Freezing Mixing

Name ____________________

Make a Model

1. These things are missing parts. Match each object to the parts that will help it move.

2. Color the three things you would need to make a wheel and axle.

3. Show how Sam can get from his house to Joey's house. Draw arrows to show the way.

Sam's House Joey's House

 Use with page E24.

Name ______________________________

What Happens When Objects Are Taken Apart?

Match each picture to the part that will make it work.

1.  • 

2. 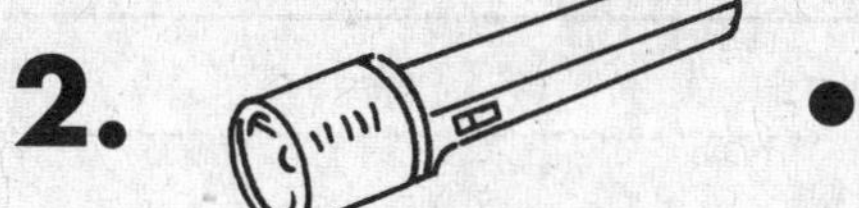 • • 

3. 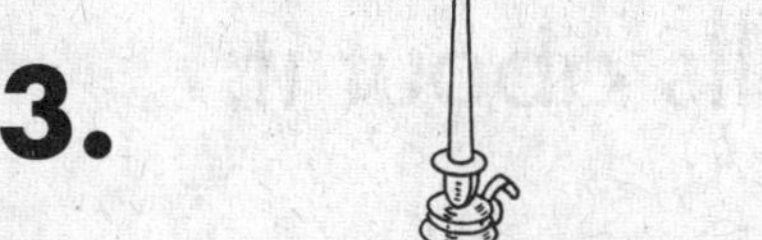 • 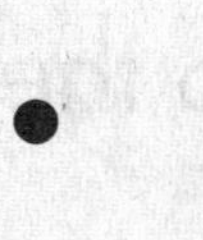

  •  

5. Mr. Smith's car does not work. Circle where he could get it fixed.

Name ______________________________

Matter

Write your answer. Use the words in the box.

gas	liquid	matter

1. I am all around you. What am I? ______________

2. I take up the shape of my container. What am I? ______________

3. I can flow fast or slow. What am I? ______________

Match the word to the picture that tells about it.

4. solids •

5. sink •

6. float •

7. change •

8. mechanic •

• 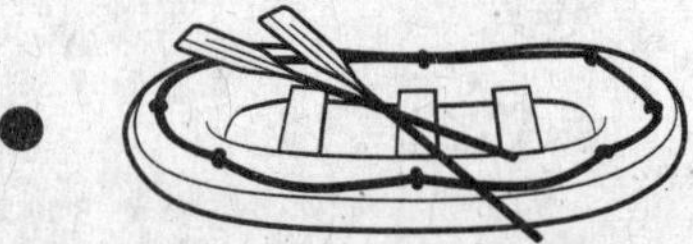

• 

• 

• 

• 

Use with pages E30–E31.

Name ______________________________

Use Numbers

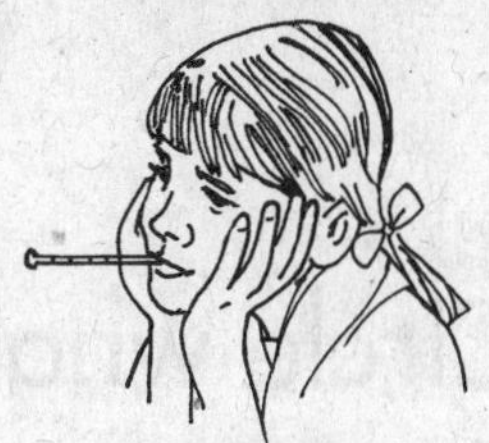

98 degrees

Record the temperature of each.

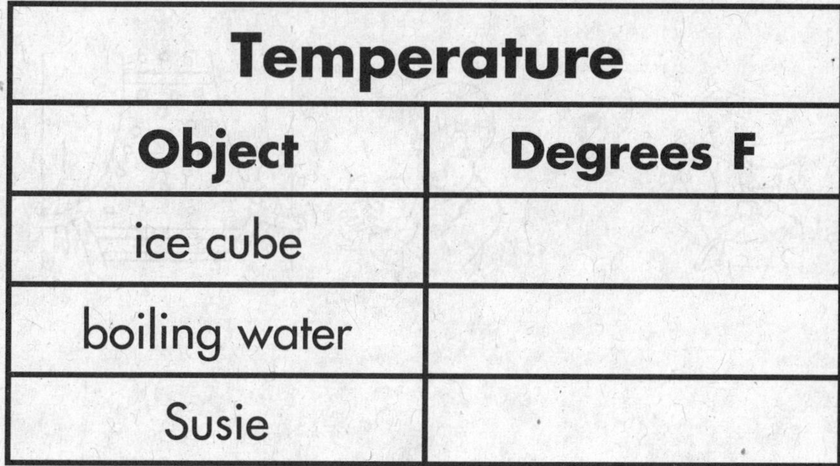

Temperature	
Object	**Degrees F**
ice cube	
boiling water	
Susie	

32 degrees

212 degrees

1. Which is the warmest?

____

2. Which is the coolest?

____

3. What happened to the temperature of the ice cube after it was in the window?

____

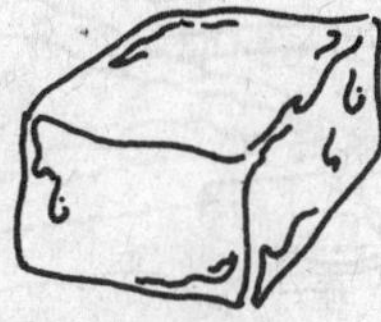

32 degrees

40 degrees

Name ______________________________

What Is Heat?

Circle what is giving each person heat.

1. 2.

3.

4. Color all the things being warmed by the sun.

Use with page E37.

Name ___________________________

Gather and Record Data

1. Circle the things that give off heat.

2. Record your data in the chart.

Objects	
Gives off heat	**Does NOT give off heat**

Use with page E38.

Name ________________________________

How Does Heat Change Matter?

Match to tell how heat changes matter.

1.  •

2.  •

3.  •

• heats the air so it spreads out and fills the balloon

• makes a solid melt

• changes liquid to a gas

4. Observe both pictures. Tell what happened.

____

____

____

Harcourt

Use with page E41.

Name ______________________________

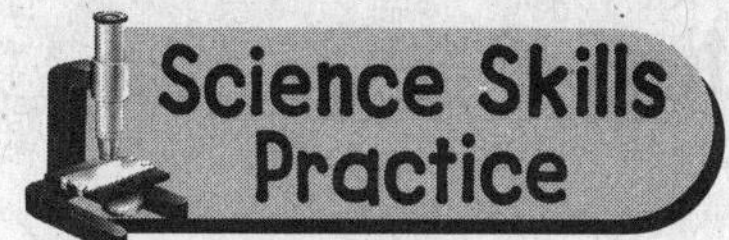

Communicate

1. Color this rainbow. Show four different colors.

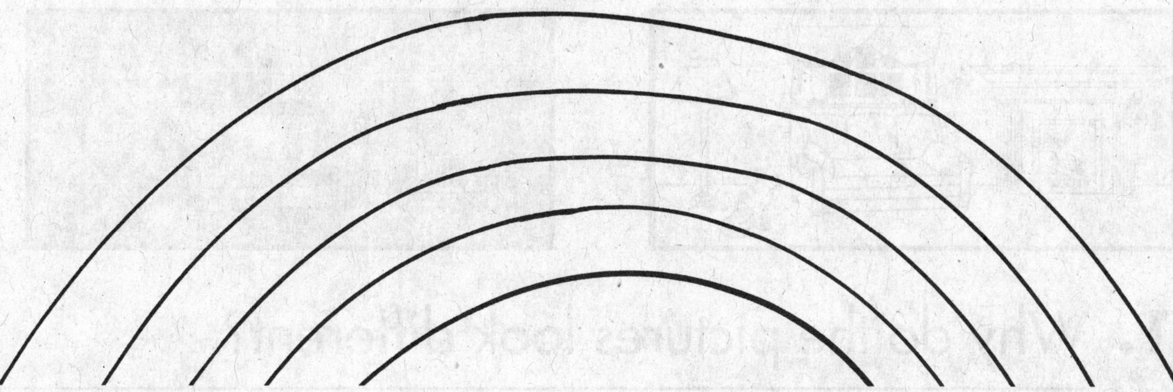

2. Color this vase and flowers. Make each flower a different color. Tell how the flowers look different.

Name ______________________________

What Is Light?

These pictures are of the same place.

1. Why do the pictures look different?

____

____

2. Circle the things that give off light. Put an **X** on the things that give off heat.

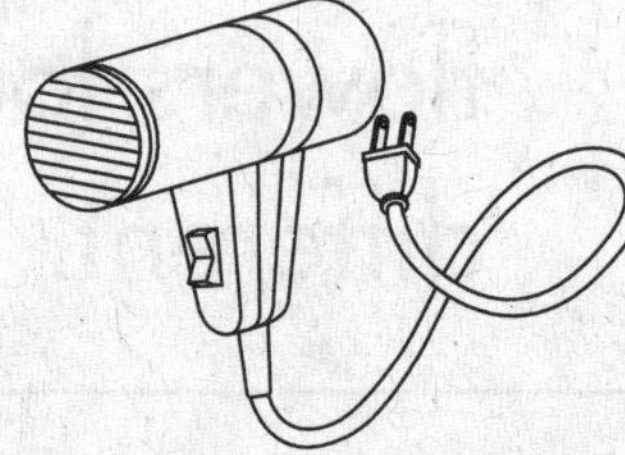

Circle the word that best finishes each sentence.

3. Light is made of _____.

the sun colors

4. A _____ breaks light into colors.

prism glass

Use with page E45.

Name ______________________________

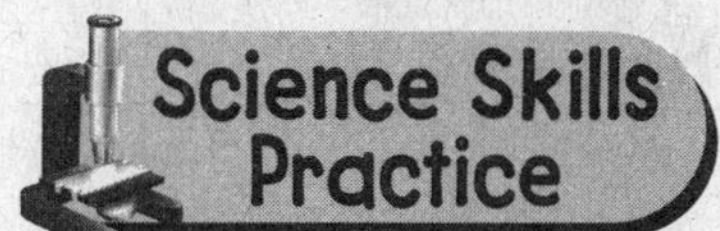

Investigate a Problem

1. This flashlight is aimed at a wall. The **X** shows where the light hits the wall. Draw an arrow to show the path the light takes to the wall.

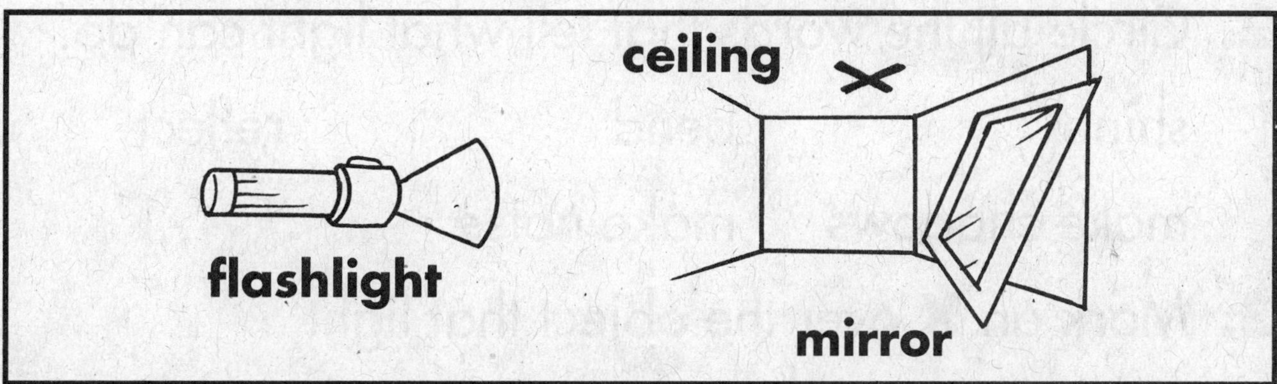

2. This flashlight is facing a mirror. The **X** shows where the light is shining. Draw arrows to show how the light gets to the ceiling.

Name ____________________

What Can Light Do?

1. Light is reflecting off this tree. **Color** the tree. Use **black** to color the shadow.

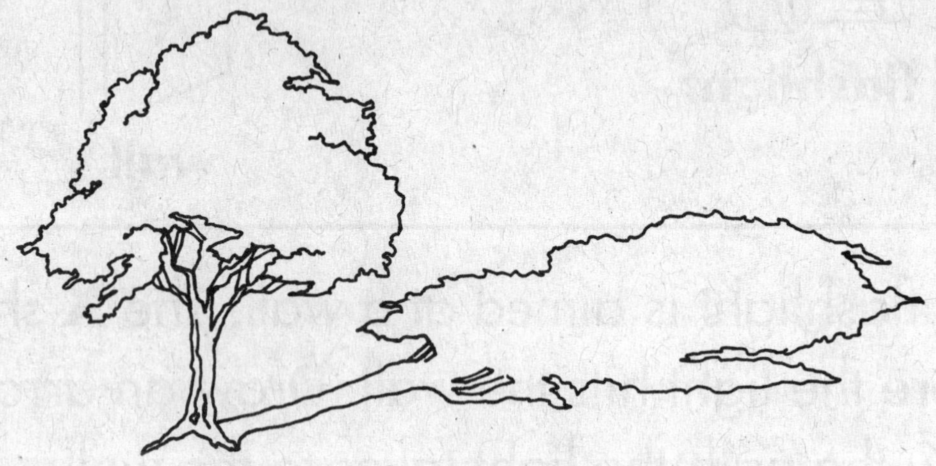

2. Circle all the words that tell what light can do.

shine bend reflect

make shadows make noise

3. Mark an **X** over the object that light can pass through.

Use with page E49.

Name ______________________________

Vocabulary Review

Heat and Light

These sentences are false. Change the underlined word to make the sentence true.

1. When solids melt they turn to a <u>gas.</u>

____

2. Electric bulbs give off <u>heat</u> to help us see.

____

3. Match the picture to the word.

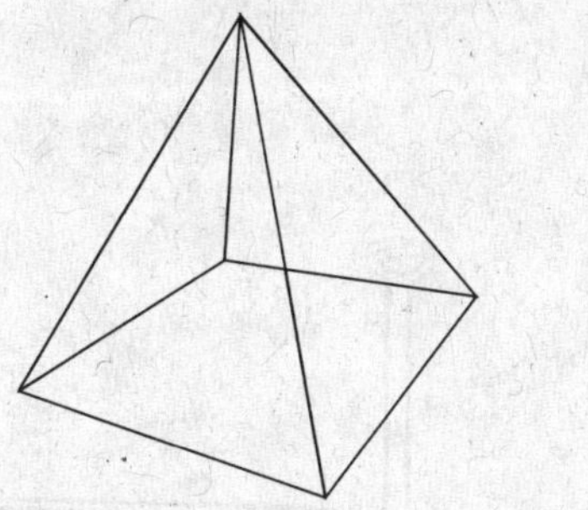

• • refract

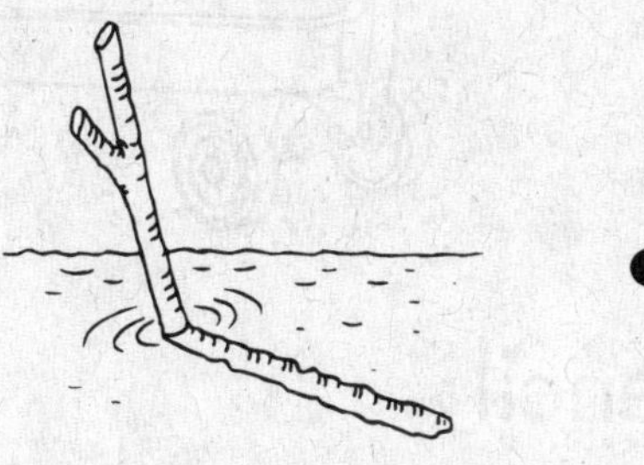

• • reflect

• • prism

Name ______________________________

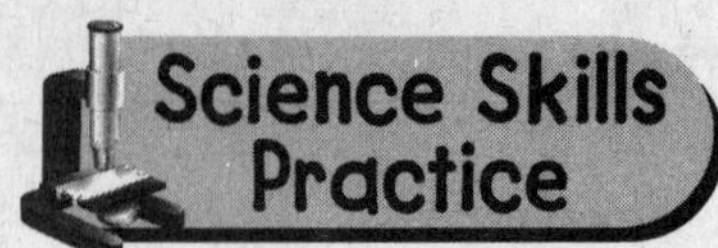

Investigate

These logs need to be moved from the pile to the campfire.

1. Circle the things that could help you move the logs.

2. Tell how you could move a pencil across a desk.

____

____

Harcourt

Use with page F4.

senses

living

nonliving

roots

living

People are **living** things.

Unit A • Chapter 1

senses

see
hear
touch
smell
taste

You use your **senses** to see, hear, smell, touch, and taste.

Unit A • Chapter 1

roots

roots

Water is taken into a plant through its **roots.**

Unit A • Chapter 2

nonliving

Rocks and air are **nonliving** things.

Unit A • Chapter 1

stem

leaves

flowers

seed

leaves

leaves

A plant makes food in its **leaves**.

Unit A • Chapter 2

stem

stem

A **stem** helps hold up a plant.

Unit A • Chapter 2

seed

A plant grows from a **seed**.

Unit A • Chapter 2

flowers

flowers

Seeds form in **flowers**.

Unit A • Chapter 2

seed coat

sunlight

gills

mammal

sunlight

Light from the sun is **sunlight**.

Unit A • Chapter 2

seed coat

seed coat

The **seed coat** covers the seed.

Unit A • Chapter 2

mammal

A dog is a **mammal**.

Unit A • Chapter 3

gills

gills

The **gills** of a fish take air from water.

Unit A • Chapter 3

reptile

amphibian

insect

hatch

amphibian

A frog is an **amphibian**.

Unit A • Chapter 3

reptile

A snake is a **reptile**.

Unit A • Chapter 3

hatch

Chicks **hatch** from eggs.

Unit A • Chapter 3

insect

An ant is an **insect**.

Unit A • Chapter 3

larva

tadpoles

pupa

shelter

pupa

A caterpillar becomes a **pupa** before it becomes a butterfly.

Unit A • Chapter 3

larva

A butterfly **larva** hatches from an egg.

Unit A • Chapter 3

shelter

A chipmunk finds **shelter** in a hollow tree.

Unit B • Chapter 1

tadpoles

A young frog, or **tadpole**, hatches from an egg.

Unit A • Chapter 3

product

enrich

forest

pollen

pollen

Bees move **pollen** from one flower to another.

Unit B • Chapter 1

enrich

An earthworm's wastes **enrich** the soil.

Unit B • Chapter 1

forest

Many trees grow in a **forest**.

Unit B • Chapter 2

product

Mittens are a **product** made from wool.

Unit B • Chapter 1

desert	rain forest
ocean	algae

rain forest

A **rain forest** is warm and wet all year.

Unit B • Chapter 2

desert

A **desert** gets lots of sunlight and little rain.

Unit B • Chapter 2

algae

Ocean plants are **algae**.

Unit B • Chapter 2

ocean

The **ocean** is filled with salt water.

Unit B • Chapter 2

soil

rock

texture

sand

Harcourt

sand

At the beach, the ground is often covered with **sand**.

Unit C • Chapter 1

rock

Some walls are made of **rock**.

Unit C • Chapter 1

texture

Eggshells and plums have a smooth **texture**.

Unit C • Chapter 1

soil

Plants grow in **soil**.

Unit C • Chapter 1

air

fresh water

stream

river

fresh water

Water in most lakes, streams, and rivers is **fresh water**.

Unit C • Chapter 2

air

You breathe **air**. It is all around you.

Unit C • Chapter 2

river

A **river** is larger than a stream.

Unit C • Chapter 2

stream

A **stream** is smaller than a river.

Unit C • Chapter 2

weather

lake

temperature

salt water

salt water

Ocean **salt water** is too salty to drink.

Unit C • Chapter 2

lake

You can swim in a **lake**.

Unit C • Chapter 2

temperature

The **temperature** may drop to freezing tonight.

Unit D • Chapter 1

weather

Snow, rain, and sunshine are different kinds of **weather**.

Unit D • Chapter 1

thermometer

wind

water cycle

evaporate

wind

Sailboats are pushed by the **wind**.

Unit D • Chapter 1

thermometer

Use a **thermometer** to measure temperature.

Unit D • Chapter 1

evaporate

The water in a puddle will **evaporate** when the sun comes out.

Unit D • Chapter 1

water cycle

The **water cycle** is how water moves from Earth to sky and back again.

Unit D • Chapter 1

water vapor

condense

season

spring

condense

Water vapor will
condense and change
to tiny drops of water.

Unit D • Chapter 1

water vapor

Water vapor is
invisible in the
air around you.

Unit D • Chapter 1

spring

April and May are
two months of **spring**.

Unit D • Chapter 2

season

My favorite **season**
is winter.

Unit D • Chapter 2

summer

fall

winter

matter

Harcourt

fall

In **fall**, leaves may turn color.

Unit D • Chapter 2

summer

The hottest time of year is **summer**.

Unit D • Chapter 2

matter

Everything around you is made of **matter**.

Unit E • Chapter 1

winter

In many places, **winter** is cold and snowy.

Unit D • Chapter 2

solid

liquid

float

sink

Harcourt

liquid

Juice is a **liquid**. It takes the shape of its container.

Unit E • Chapter 1

solid

A table is a **solid**.

Unit E • Chapter 1

sink

A weight will **sink** to the bottom of the tank.

Unit E • Chapter 1

float

A boat will **float** on the water.

Unit E • Chapter 1

gas

change

mechanic

heat

change

A person can **change** the clay.

Unit E • Chapter 1

gas

Air is a **gas**.

Unit E • Chapter 1

heat

The sun's **heat** warms the air.

Unit E • Chapter 2

mechanic

Mrs. Jones is a **mechanic** who fixes airplanes.

Unit E • Chapter 1

reflects

melt

refract

prism

prism

A **prism** breaks light into colors.

Unit E • Chapter 2

melt

Heat can make ice cream **melt**.

Unit E • Chapter 2

refract

Light can bend, or **refract**.

Unit E • Chapter 2

reflects

Light **reflects** off objects that you see.

Unit E • Chapter 2

force

push

pull

zigzag

push

You **push** a football when you throw it.

Unit F • Chapter 1

force

A push is a **force**.

Unit F • Chapter 1

zigzag

A skater can **zigzag** across the ice.

Unit F • Chapter 1

pull

You **pull** a wagon to move it.

Unit F • Chapter 1

friction

motion

wheel

surface

surface

A table has a flat **surface**.

Unit F • Chapter 1

motion

The **motion** of a merry-go-round is in a circle.

Unit F • Chapter 1

wheel

A **wheel** turns and the toy moves easily.

Unit F • Chapter 1

friction

The sand on the road gives the car more **friction**.

Unit F • Chapter 1

magnet

attract

strength

poles

attract

A magnet will **attract** objects made of iron.

Unit F • Chapter 2

magnet

A **magnet** holds papers on the refrigerator.

Unit F • Chapter 2

poles

A magnet is strongest at its **poles**.

Unit F • Chapter 2

strength

A magnet can have a lot of **strength**.

Unit F • Chapter 2

repel

magnetic
force

magnetize

magnetic force

A **magnetic force** attracts the paper clips to the magnet.

Unit F • Chapter 2

repel

Like poles of two magnets **repel**.

Unit F • Chapter 2

magnetize

A magnet can **magnetize** iron objects.